CW00920149

OUTDOOR LONDON

GREEN SPACES AND ESCAPES IN AND AROUND THE CAPITAL

BY ELEANOR ROSS

PHOTOGRAPHS BY CAMILLE MACK

WHITE LION PUBLISHING

CONTENTS

INTRODUCTION

Monet painted London as a city of dappled light, greens, yellows, oranges, browns, and blues. At first glance the city seems grey, but spend longer than five minutes in the capital and you realise it's easy to duck out, away from the capital's congested roads, to find green spaces and ponds that look like they were painted by Claude himself. It's a multi-layered city, one packed with ways to lose oneself, whether that's on a hike, in a kayak, on a train heading out to the nearby Surrey Hills, or plunging into a cool, refreshing pond at the height of summer.

London has a reputation for being fast-paced and always-on, which is why Londoners appreciate the secluded spaces and slithers of tiny parks that the city provides. Visitors and locals alike need no excuse to head outside.

This guide goes beyond the parks that everyone's heard of. Hyde Park, Regents Park, and St James's Park are brilliant, beautiful spaces, and are well known for good reason. But what about London's other green spaces, such as the Parkland Walk, which leads, like a ribbon of forest, through residential north London towards Hampstead Heath? Or St Dunstan in the East, a secluded, bombed-out church that even in winter is a place of meditative quiet in the heart of the city? The parks, walks, bike-rides and swimming spots in the following sections are a mix of well-known and local favourites.

London's ecological diversity in particular can come as a welcome surprise for visitors. Who would have thought that in a city once famed for its pea-souper smogs and docklands industry, there are opportunities to spot eels, bees, newts and hedgehogs in one of the London Wildlife Trust's 41 nature reserves across the capital? From plant-crammed balconies to guerilla gardening (where Londoners take over kerbs and disused flower beds), it's clear us locals love a bit of green. And who can blame us? Councils install free park-gyms for residents to use, while new cycle routes and paths are popping up all over the place. Greater London is increasingly becoming a green city, with its 8 million trees and 47 per cent of land taken up by parks and green-space.

After industrialisation in the nineteenth century, ancient hunting grounds like Richmond Park and Epping Forest were swallowed up by the city, leaving swathes of green in otherwise built-up grey areas. The result is lots of parks, secret spaces, wild pockets and easy-to-hike walks and bike rides around the city. Getting lost in London doesn't need to stop at walking either. The city is also jam-packed with rivers, ponds and lidos, many of which are navigable. Swim, kayak or paddleboard through London in the humid summer to keep heat at bay, and explore the city from a different angle. So, dive in, and follow the tree line to sink into London at its greenest.

PARKS

PARKS

A 'green city', in just 70 square miles Greater London has more than 1,700 parks, all of which are open to the public and free to explore. Whether you want to get away from the chaos and immerse yourself in nature or simply need somewhere to walk your dog, London has a park for everyone. Some, such as Hyde Park and Regent's Park, in central London, are already well known and much visited by locals and tourists alike, while others like Vauxhall Pleasure Gardens or Southwark Park, in central south-east London, have more of a community vibe. Whether you're going mainstream or off the beaten track, pack a picnic hamper and some sunnies and get ready to discover some of London's greenest places.

✿ ALEXANDRA PALACE

A hilltop haven on a hot day, north London's iconic Alexandra Palace has some of the most spectacular views of the city. More affectionately known today as 'Ally Pally', it opened in 1873, a pleasure park for London's rapidly growing population to let off steam. It follows the traditional Victorian layout for parks tightly. There are ornamental gardens, a boating lake and plenty of green space and woodland to conjure up the illusion that you're not really in the city at all, just merely observing the busy city below. The original Alexandra Palace burned down in 1873, but was replaced in 1875. Today, it fulfils its original intention of being a 'People's Palace' – as a premier venue, it's a building used for entertaining the masses. The park also has an ice rink and a conservation area. It's great for kids to get lost in and for adults just to stretch out and enjoy their surroundings on a lovely sunny day.

—

Alexandra Palace Way, London N22 7AY

www.alexandrapalace.com

Opening times: 24 hours

Getting there: ⊖ Wood Green (Piccadilly), Finsbury Park (Victoria); ⇝ Alexandra Palace

✿ VAUXHALL PLEASURE GARDENS

In its heyday, Vauxhall Pleasure Gardens was so illustrious that Handel's *Music for the Royal Fireworks* was first staged here, celebrating the fireworks display of 1749. In the 1780s, visitors would cross London to view a hot air balloon tethered there take to the skies, and ride the funfair and watch high society at play. Today, the gardens are a much more modest affair. In the autumn, when the trees burn gold, it's still a glorious place to stroll through on the way to the Black Dog pub, which serves some great craft beers, or have a Bloody Mary and a slice of cake at the cosy Tea House Theatre. Animal lovers will enjoy horse riding in the paddocks developed with nearby Vauxhall City Farm and feeding the goats and alpacas that kick up dust in summer, while the clink of boules adds a slice of gentile civility in summer as London Petanque Club practises curving throws across the grass.

—

Tyers Street, London SE11 5HL
Opening times: 24 hours
Getting there: ⊖ Vauxhall (Victoria); ⇌ Vauxhall

✿ MILE END PARK

After the war, a huge clean-up operation was required in east London, and Mile End Park grew out of that destruction. The towers of Canary Wharf are visible from much of the 76-acre park, which is separated by the Hertford Union Canal from the south edge of Victoria Park. It also follows the Regent's Canal from Victoria Park to Limehouse Basin. Among the many attractions are the Art Pavilion, a beautiful gallery overlooking a pretty duck pond, and the award-winning Green Bridge which has a footpath lined with trees and feels more New York High Line than Stepney. The Children's Park is fabulously equipped, with climbing walls, an extensive playground, a well-maintained sandpit and rope swing, as well as playground equipment for disabled and able-bodied children.

—

Clinton Rd, London E3 4QY
Opening times: 24 hours
Getting there: ⊖ Mile End (Central)

🌸 HOLLAND PARK

Holland Park, in west London, is the sort of place you visit and just sigh because it's so lovely. Verges are trimmed and grass is Wimbledon-green. Take your pick from the Dutch Garden – lined with vibrant orange and purple flower beds, perfuming the pavements with lavender and the dahlias that the Earl of Holland's wife grew first in England – or the Kyoto Gardens, created as a gesture of friendship in 1991 by Kyoto's Chamber of Commerce. Bonsai trees, neatly trimmed, are reflected in the still koi carp pond and a *karesansui*, a traditional Japanese rock garden, tumbles down a man-made hill. Where the hard paths fall away and are replaced by soft tracks running through beech and birch trees there's a sprawl of wilderness. The kids adventure playground is one of the best free play parks in the city, with its giant tyre swing and long zipwire. For adults, the Design Museum to the park's south-east is worth a browse, if only to gawp at the striking roof and airy atrium.

—

Ilchester Pl, London W8 6LU

Opening times: 7:30am to 30 minutes before dusk

Getting there: ⊖ Holland Park (Central), Kensington High Street (Circle/District)

❀ CRYSTAL PALACE PARK

'There be dinosaurs here' is perhaps not something you might expect to hear in south-east London. Yet, in the bowels of Crystal Palace Park, 30 dinosaurs can be found climbing hills, next to ponds and peeking out from behind trees. Even though this feels like a modern art installation, the Grade I-listed dinosaurs date back to 1854 and were built by Benjamin Waterhouse Hawkins when Crystal Palace was still described as a 'pleasure ground'. Remnants of the 1851 Great Exhibition can be found scattered across the park – gigantic terraces, stone sphinx statues and fountains. Adults and kids alike can get lost in the 160-foot maze, one of the largest in the country; free to enter, the centre is surprisingly difficult to find. Hunt out the park café for a brew and biscuits, a perfect place to rest if you're incorporating the park into a longer walk: the park is part of the 50-mile Green Chain walk, but can also be included in a lovely wooded section of the long-distance path between the Horniman Museum and Sydenham Hill Woods.

—

42 Thicket Rd, London SE19 2GA

www.crystalpalacepark.org.uk

Opening times: 7:30am–dusk

Getting there: ⇌ Crystal Palace; Penge West

✿ BATTERSEA PARK

Battersea Park is a great example of Victorian working design – park planners were given a slither of green space and encouraged to fill it with 'amusements' that would help local residents relax after the daily grind. Those amusements still exist and are popular with local families, and tourists alike, who enjoy the pedalos on the landscaped boating lake, the Pump House Gallery, a bandstand (hosting live music during summer) and ornamental gardens. There's also a tremendous view of Albert Bridge, lit at night with 4,000 LED lamps glittering over the river. Kids will love Go Ape, a tree-top high-octane rope course.

Add astroturf pitches, acres of parkland and a riverside location and you have a sparkling gem of a park that visitors and locals cherish. The focal point is the 33.5m high peace pagoda, built by monks, nuns and followers of Nipponzan Myōhōji Buddhist order. A south London beacon, it is somewhere for people to meet and joggers to run towards as the evening sun casts long shadows on the south-side of the Thames.

Queenstown Road, London SW11 4NJ
www.wandsworth.gov.uk/batterseapark
Opening times: 8am–dusk
Getting there: ⇌ Battersea Park

✿ CLISSOLD PARK

Seven gates mark seven different entrances to Clissold Park, a sprawling 23-hectares between Arsenal to the west, Stoke Newington to the east and Hackney to the north-west. Gifted to the public in 1889, there are enough attractions here to keep the entire family interested. A soft-on-the-knees bark athletics track encircles the park, while kids on scooters tear down paths that criss-cross the large expanse of green grass. Spires and roofs from Stoke Newington's Church Street peek out over the tops of the park's beech trees and, in summer, the full foliage makes it feel like you're in the heart of the Cotswolds rather than Zone 2. It's big enough to lose yourself in, but small enough to return to city life when you're ready. Festivals, from craft fairs to races, run throughout the year, while inner-city wildlife spotters are also in for a treat – deer have roamed Clissold Park since the 1890s, while an aviary and local species butterfly dome mean parakeets and other brightly coloured insects flit overhead.

—

Green Lanes, London N16 9HJ
www.clissoldpark.com
Opening times: 7:30am–9pm
Getting there: ⊖ Finsbury Park (Victoria);
⇌ Stoke Newington

✿ VICTORIA PARK

A behemoth of a park in the heart of east
London, Victoria Park is perhaps best-known for
its massive capacity gigs and huge multi-day
festivals like All Points East. But, 'Vicky Park',
as it's known by locals, is packed with so much
more than just the odd summer festival. Rowing
boats and pedalos can be rented to explore the
lake, while those interested in local history can
follow the Memoryscape trail. Kids won't be
disappointed with the playgrounds either – the
V&A playground has sandboxes, swings and even
water pumps to encourage creative play, while
The Hub and The Splash have climbing walls and
fountains for kids to cool off in during summer.
The park's so big that there are three park walking
routes called Tree Walks, which jump from tree
species to tree species, taking in boulevards,
sailing ponds and ending at the Park Café run by
Cyrus Todiwala, which serves a now infamous
(and delicious) Indian breakfast.

—

Grove Rd, London E3 5TB
www.towerhamlets.gov.uk/lgnl/leisure_and_culture/
parks_and_open_spaces/victoria_park/victoria_park.aspx
Opening times: 7am–dusk
Getting there: ⊖ Mile End (Central);
⇌ Cambridge Heath/Hackney Wick

✿ RICHMOND PARK

One of the eight Royal Parks, Richmond Park is vast and beautiful. At three times the size of New York's Central Park, this 2,500-acre park wears a lot of different badges, from National Nature Reserve to Site of Special Scientific Interest. The 40-acre woodland Isabella Plantation garden features beautiful azaleas and rare trees and plants. Get there on an early autumn morning to see magnificent stags rutting in the mist, fighting for the attention of females. Richmond Park is well-equipped for bike rides and there's a 7.5-mile loop (Tamsin Trail) that runs around the entire park, for hikers and cyclists alike. Hunt down King Henry's Mound (Henry VIII allegedly stood here, waiting for the sign that Anne Boleyn had been beheaded), where you can peer through a telescope and see all the way to St Paul's Cathedral, 12 miles away, through a gap in the trees. No building is allowed to impede it – the view is officially protected for eternity.

—

Richmond
www.royalparks.org.uk/parks/richmond-park
Opening times: Pedestrian gates open 24 hours;
vehicle gates open 7am until dusk
Getting there: ⊖ Richmond (District); ⇌ Richmond

🌸 THAMES BARRIER PARK

To celebrate the creation of the largest riverside park built in London in 50 years, landscape architects cultivated well-manicured hedges that undulate towards the water, as if creating a meeting point between ground and river.

The park, with its 130-foot long sunken garden, 32 fountains, wide walkways and post-modern design is a gorgeous sunspot to relax in by the water. A pavilion of remembrance, celebrating the lives of those who died in the Second World War, stands next to the river, but it's the Thames Barrier itself that dwarfs the park. Originally built to protect the city from North Sea storm surges and high tides, it can be opened and closed depending on how high the tide is. This magnificent feat of engineering is complemented by the park's 14 acres of straight edges, rainbow flower borders and magnificent concrete trench.

—

Barrier Point Road, London E16 2HP
www.gardenvisit.com/gardens/thames_barrier_park
Opening times: 7am; closing times vary by month
Getting there: ⇌ Pontoon Dock DLR

26

🌸 GUNNERSBURY PARK

In 1925, Mrs de Rothschild sold west London-located Gunnersbury Park to the nation, on the condition that its 200 hectares only be used for leisure. The park is dominated by a listed Georgian Palladian mansion and follies and historic ruins abound – an eighteenth-century folly overlooks the Potomac boating pond, while the Orangery and remnants of an eighteenth-century bathhouse built by Princess Amelia, George II's daughter, are keen reminders of the park's illustrious heritage. Today it's a large, attractive space for festivals, such as Lovebox and Citadel, making the most of the flat, green space. There's also a pitch and putt, football pitches and a promise that the park will receive millions of pounds of funds for sports-related regeneration.

—

Gunnersbury Park, Popes Lane, London W3 8LQ
www.visitgunnersbury.org
Opening times: 8am–dusk
Getting there: ⊖ Acton Town (Piccadilly/District), South Ealing (Piccadilly); ⇌ Kew Bridge

✿ LONDON FIELDS

Hackney's London Fields used to be a public common and a place where farmers and their sheep could rest as they walked to London's markets. Now bordered by the ever-popular Broadway Market to the south, it's usually packed with young people making the most of the nearby food stalls. Within the 31 acres or so of green space, the park is home to one of London's only heated outdoor lidos, a cricket pitch at its centre, play areas for kids with energy to burn, and wildflower meadows that are home to local honeybee hives. For foodie offerings away from the market, there is the laid-back Pub on the Park, which has a chilled beer garden in summer, and open fires come winter. Uniquely, London Fields is one of the only parks in London where barbecues are permitted, with a designated grilling spot.

—

London Fields West Side, Hackney, London E8 3EU
www.hackney.gov.uk/london-fields
Opening times: 24 hours
Getting there: ⇌ London Fields

✿ BURGESS PARK

This wedge of park sitting between Camberwell and Old Kent Road is one of south London's largest parks at 56 hectares. Created from old bomb-sites after the Second World War, it's cut through by The Surrey Canal Tree Walk, which follows the old canal and highlights edible plants and trees, including crab apples, damsons and sweet chestnuts, along the route for budding foragers. Come summer, wisps of smoke from barbecues trail above the hillocks, as families decamp with friends on the grass. Home to park runs, bike paths and the odd moorhen, this is a welcome relief from some of south London's more congested spaces.

—

150 Albany Rd, London SE5 0AL

Opening times: 24 hours

Getting there: ⊖ Elephant and Castle (Bakerloo)

🌸 BROCKWELL PARK

Packed with parents and prams, running fanatics and more outdoor yoga classes than you can shake a stick at, Brockwell Park sits between fashionable Brixton and family-oriented Herne Hill. There's a bandstand, a large duck pond and even a miniature steam train run by toy railway enthusiasts. One of the park's biggest draws is the lido; built in 1937, it's a 50m unheated outside pool on the southern edge of the park. As well as swimming, you can do yoga, tai chi and pilates classes. It's so popular that queues can wend for hundreds of metres in the summer. The Lido Café is well worth visiting, the brunches sublime. The park is becoming a hotspot for summer music festivals. The Lambeth Country Show is held here each year, so you can weigh animals and hang out with cows even in London's Zone 2.

—

Norwood Rd, London SE24 9BJ
Opening times: 7:30am–dusk
Getting there: ⊖ Brixton (Victoria line); ⇌ Herne Hill

✿ VAUXHALL PARK

This tiny park packs a big punch. From the outside it looks like a standard neighbourhood dog-walking park – and mostly, it is – but a few things set it apart from all the other squares of green scattered around the city. One is that one of the park's founders was the great Suffragist Millicent Fawcett; another is that to the south of the park is a lavender field, rivalling those in Provence for colour and smell. Fat bees hum over the plants all summer and, at harvest, volunteers meet and press thousands of flowers to create the litres of lavender oil sold by the Friends of Vauxhall Park at Italo, in Bonnington Square. The strands of lavender grow so high and smell so sweet that it's the perfect place for nestling down with a paperback. There's also a charming model village, two tennis courts and a small playground for kids, all making it a lovely spot to while away a few hours. The park has also won the prestigious Green Flag Award, which is given to the best green spaces in the country.

—

12 Lawn Lane, London SW8 1UA
www.vauxhallpark.org.uk
Opening times: 8:30am–6pm weekdays;
10am–6pm weekends
Getting there: ⊖ Vauxhall (Victoria)

❀ MORDEN HALL PARK

In winter, a mist softens the rays of sun trying to penetrate through the oak trees in Morden Hall Park which creates a yellow, otherworldly hue. There are over 50 hectares of parkland to explore in this National Trust property, including the rose garden, home to some 2,000 varieties of roses. The secluded garden bursts with surprises, from the statues of Venus and Neptune in the rose garden to the flowing stream of the River Wandle, where it surfaces on its journey north towards the Thames. The garden used to be the site of an old tobacco factory, and today an old snuff mill stands in the gardens, complete with a millstone that powered the mill. The Park is a cracking space, feeling more like countryside than south London. For snacks and other facilities try the Potting Shed Café, which does a mean cream tea on the banks of the River Wandle.

—

Morden Hall Park, Morden, Surrey, SM4 5JD
www.nationaltrust.org.uk/morden-hall-park
Opening times: 8am–6pm
Getting there: ⊖ Morden (Northern); ⚊ tram to Phipps Bridge

✿ HAGGERSTON PARK

Located between Haggerston, Bethnal Green and Broadway Market, Haggerston Park, in south-west Hackney, is one of those places where, on each visit, there's something new to find. You might stumble across wild scrubland, perfect for rambling and dog walks. There's the hidden duck pond surrounded by reeds and then there's a huge lawned section of the park, hidden behind an 8-feet high brick wall. In true east London style, the park is littered with quirky statues, and an ancient vine twists its way along a concrete pergola. In summer, this Green Flag-awarded park is packed with sun-seeking locals. As well as wild space, there are BMX tracks, football pitches and basketball courts, while the children's play area is fine for weekend adventures. A community orchard and raised food beds also point to a local food-growing movement. There are plenty of pockets of woodland to explore and get lost in around the park.

—

Yorkton St, London E2 8NH
www.hackney.gov.uk/haggerston-park
Opening times: 7:30am–dusk
Getting there: ⊖ Bethnal Green (Central);
⇌ Haggerston Overland

GARDENS

GARDENS

London's gardens act as havens for Londoners needing respite from a busy city. To find the best ones, you often need to check out the most unusual places - whether that's the top floors of skyscrapers or inside concrete buildings. Wherever you are, there's probably a garden secreted away somewhere nearby - built in an old shipping container, grown alongside an old railway or behind an unassuming brick wall. Take the time to peer around corners and it's likely you'll be horticulturally rewarded - London is full of surprises.

❀ CONSERVATORY, BARBICAN

From the outside you'd never guess this concrete structure in east London contained anything green at all. Yet within this temple of brutalism, the 2,000 plants and tropical trees soften the angles in the Barbican Conservatory. It's a towering space with huge windows semi-covered with vines, and girders and concrete draped in ivy. It's humid too, with shoals of koi carp swimming in the shadows of the wide, green-leafed banana plants that make it feel more like the equator than central London. Keep your eyes peeled for the terrapins which were relocated from Hampstead Heath to live out their days safe from children and foxes. Open on select Sundays and Bank Holidays, the conservatory also offers afternoon tea. Book for some top cake and sandwiches served with a healthy splash of Prosecco.

—

Level 3, Barbican Centre, Silk Street, London EC2Y 8DS
www.barbican.org.uk/whats-on/2018/event/
conservatory
Opening times: 12pm–5pm (last entry 4:30pm) on
select Sundays and Bank Holidays
Getting there: ⊖ Barbican (Northern), St Pauls
(Central), Moorgate (Hammersmith & City/
Metropolitan); ⇌ Moorgate, Liverpool Street,
Farringdon

❀ HAMPTON COURT PALACE GARDENS

You can only use superlatives when describing Hampton Court Palace's riverside gardens. It has the oldest maze, the longest mixed flower border and the largest vine. Until recently the maze was one of the biggest draws for visitors to Henry VIII's former home, but other features such as William III and Mary II's elegant Great Fountain Garden hold as many treasures. For kids, The Magic Garden, full of mythical beasts and a secret grotto, is unmissable. It's not so much a physical garden but an interactive, fun, learning experience deep within the grounds of the Palace. There is also 'Capability' Brown's 250-year-old Great Vine, its longest branch 36m. The grapes are so sweet and bursting with flavour that Queen Victoria used to have them sent to her at her residences at Windsor and on the Isle of White – lucky for us non-royals, it was decreed that the public could buy the excess crop in the early nineteenth century. The rest of the gardens are a mix of ornate topiary, extravagant fountains and vivacious herbaceous borders.

—

East Molesey, Surrey KT8 9AU
www.hrp.org.uk
Opening times: 10am–6pm (last admission 5:15pm to The Magic Garden/Maze)
Get there: ⇌ Hampton Court Station

🌸 ST GEORGE'S GARDENS

This is the beating soul of Bloomsbury, in central London, with gardens surrounded by tall white houses and university buildings. Tombstones line the back walls of the square – although there's no church, this central London space was once the burial grounds for St George's Bloomsbury and St George's Holborn and remains consecrated ground. It was turned into gardens to 'bring beauty home to the poor' in 1884. Today, it is popular with office workers looking for a peaceful place to eat a sandwich and tourists wanting to rest their feet. Still, the gardens remain the final resting place for some interesting characters, including Eliza Fenning, a cook who tried to poison her employers, subsequently executed, Oliver Cromwell's favourite daughter and 10 Jacobites, hung, drawn and quartered at Kennington Park's Surrey Gallows in 1746. Today, the park features a variety of ferns and is scattered with benches, carved stone angels and old grave plinths. It's a place for quiet, peaceful reflection, an oasis in the centre of London.

—

62 Marchmont Street, London WC1N 6BN
www.friendsofstgeorgesgardens.org.uk
Opening times: 7:30am–8:15pm
Getting there: ⊖ Russell Square (Piccadilly)

✿ BONNINGTON SQUARE GARDEN

A slice of egalitarian living in Vauxhall, Bonnington Square has attracted a free-thinking alternative crowd since the 1980s. The surrounding houses, made up of tall terraces dating from the 1870s, were earmarked for demolition by the City of London in the 1970s. Squatters moved in and founded a housing cooperative and a volunteer-led vegetarian café. A group of local residents, including gardener Dan Pearson, transformed the bombed-out space at the centre into a garden. Today, it is still tended to by community volunteers. In summer, local kids can often be seen getting their hands dirty weeding or exploring the hydrangeas and agapanthus. The garden is one of the most jungle-like in the city – cool, green vines climb loudly painted telegraph poles, while windowsill flowerbeds pop with colour from the front of almost every house. It's not quite the bohemian paradise of the 1980s any more, but it is without doubt, one of London's finest community gardens.

—

11C Bonnington Square, London SW8 1TF
www.bonningtonsquaregarden.org.uk
Opening times: Monday to Friday,
9:30am–7:45pm; Saturday 9:30am–2pm
Getting there: ⊖ Vauxhall (Victoria)

🌸 KEW GARDENS

Kew is the grandmother of all gardens, with some of the largest collections of plants in the world. If any new seed or plant species was discovered during a Crown expedition in the nineteenth century, this is where it was sent to and stored. Whether you're an old-hand green thumb or just wanting to get out of the big smoke for a few hours, this riverside royal botanical garden does its best to appeal to everyone. It includes an arboretum with more than 14,000 trees and a treetop walk. Scattered around the grounds, conservatories and other listed buildings jut out of trees, and striking glass walls reflect blossom and sky. The architecturally stunning Davies Alpine House provides the perfect conditions for the garden's collection of mountain-loving plants, while the magnificent Palm House encloses a miniature rainforest, complete with climbers and endangered orchids in a tropical heat. The Marianne North Gallery houses the Victorian artist's botanical paintings from her travels around the world. Kids will love the Hive, a multi-sensory, immersive experience that celebrates the life cycle of bees, with its own unique soundscape reflecting the activity of a nearby real beehive.

Richmond TW9 3AE

www.kew.org

Opening times: 10am–7pm; admission £17.75, children 4–16 £4, members/under 4s free

Getting there: ⊖ Kew Gardens (District); ⇌ Kew Bridge

🌸 KINGS CROSS SKIP GARDEN

A garden where everything is made from recycled materials *and* can be moved if needed – how brilliant is that? Run by charity Global Generation, the skip garden is made from, you guessed it, empty skips – filled with compost and bedded with edible plants and greenery. It started as a solitary skip filled with vegetables, but it's bloomed into a larger community-led project, with kids from local schools helping to weed and plant. It's not just confined to small plants either – apple trees and bean poles tower out of the skips, while polythene tunnels grow chillis, tomatoes and ginger. All gardening is organic – worms are used to compost and rain water is harvested to hydrate the beds. As this is an area of prime urban land, as it's sold on, the skip garden can be picked up and relocated if needed. All vegetables are put to good use. The garden also has an onsite kitchen specialising in seasonal vegetarian dishes.

—

1 Tapper Walk, London N1C 4AQ
www.kingscross.co.uk/skip-garden
Openning times: Tuesday to Saturday, 10am–4pm
Getting there: ⊖ Kings Cross (Northern/Victoria);
⇌ Kings Cross

🌸 DALSTON EASTERN CURVE GARDEN

East Londoners always seem to know exactly how to utilise old brownfield sites, whether that's by transforming them into food truck hangouts or, in the case of Dalston Eastern Curve Garden, into a pocket of green space. Built along a disused railway track, it is as narrow and long as you might expect. The garden does edibles well – herbs, artichokes and fruit are all grown here, alongside trees and a wilder area complete with hawthorn and wildflowers. The raised planters are full of species meant to attract bees, butterflies and wildlife to the area. Visitors who want to get a bit muddy will be thrilled to know that from 2pm on Saturdays the garden welcomes volunteers. The Curve Garden also has a staggeringly good wood-burning pizza oven, served alongside wine, cake and coffee, so you can get your daily fix and support the community at the same time. Easy.

—

13 Dalston Lane, London E8 3DF

www.dalstongarden.org

Opening times: Thursday to Sunday, 11am–7pm; Friday/Saturday 11am–10pm

Getting there: ≉ Dalston Junction

❀ THE ROOKERY

Streatham Common has a secret. Past the tree-lined playing fields, past the groups of young professionals playing ultimate frisbee and beyond the park café serving ice cream, there's a hilltop landscaped Green Flag garden known as The Rookery. At the hill's crown, there's a thick ring of beech and oak trees which open out onto a manicured lawn and wooden pergola threaded with blossoming plants. Magnolia lead you along the pergola towards a tumbling stream, complete with a fountain. Another larger pond leads to an old English manicured garden, festooned with peonies and marigolds, azaleas and Japanese bamboo, while the lawns are often used for outdoor theatre. The White Garden, opened to the public in 1913, contains, as its name suggests, only white plants, which contrast with the red brickwork and green beds. It's a walled garden and a place of peace and contemplation.

—

Covington Way, London SW16 3BX
Opening times: 7:30am–dusk
Getting there: ⇌ Streatham Common

✿ HAMPSTEAD HEATH HILL GARDEN AND PERGOLA

Overlooking the West Heath, there's a large stone pergola dominating the surrounding trees and meadows, a stunning Edwardian feature elevating the rugged lands to classical elegance. The Pergola took nearly two decades to complete and Londoners today must bless the mad dreams of the eccentric Lord Leverhulme who wanted a place to hold extravagant parties and to spend long summer nights with his friends and family. The resulting Hill Pergola is an architectural gem, which wouldn't look out of place in Tuscany, its height, structure and creation made possible by the soil dug up to build the Northern Line tube extension. Over the years, the Pergola has fallen into disrepair, but that's part of the charm. No longer the playground for north London's rich socialites, the Pergola is a proper Romeo and Juliet structure for everyone to enjoy.

—

The Pergola, Inverforth Cl, London NW3 7EX
Opening times: Dawn to dusk
Getting there: ⊖ Hampstead (Northern Line)

✿ SKY GARDEN

Located in the building known locally as 'The Walkie-Talkie', London's highest public garden involves taking a stomach-churning, breathtaking lift to the top of 20 Fenchurch Street. Ranged over three floors and with 360-degree views across London, the Sky Garden features North African and Mediterranean plants and is designed to resemble a mountain slope, although as the plants are not quite fully grown, it feels more like a rockery than a pasture. Visitors are given 1.5 hours to explore the gardens and sit and chat, but you're probably here less for the horticulture and more for the novelty of exploring or eating and drinking in a garden in the sky. It's free to visit, but just remember to book a time slot before you go.

---

20 Fenchurch Street, London EC3M 8AF
www.skygarden.london/sky-garden
Opening times: Monday to Friday, 10am–6pm; Saturday/Sunday, 11am–9pm
Getting there: ⊖ Monument (Circle/District), Bank (Central/Northern/DLR); ⇌ Fenchurch Street, Cannon Street, London Bridge

SECLUDED PLACES

SECLUDED PLACES

London's a city that's grown over thousands of years.
Roads twist and turn and footpaths loop. This results in
a city that's crammed full of secluded spaces, whether
that's forgotten churchyards or riverside community
gardens. Despite London's huge population (pushing nine
million), there's always somewhere to escape the crowds.
Many spaces are natural, while others are man-made,
celebrating the beauty of green and grey. These are
places to hide yourself away in: take a book, lie back
and listen to the birdsong above or to the chatter of
busy, busy London.

🌸 BROMPTON CEMETERY

Brompton Cemetery, in south-west London, has the Victorian melodrama of Paris's Père Lachaise Cemetery. One of the 'Magnificent Seven' garden cemeteries, it's complete with stone angels struck in agonised poses calling to God for forgiveness and winged stone creatures praying for redemption. Both moving and somewhat macabre, it's a lovely spot to while away a few hours, particularly in summer when you can watch the sun warm up the 35,000 or so monuments. The heady scent of yew trees perfumes the air around the benches, pushed back against tall walls or set out in circles. It has many famous residents, such as Suffragette Emmeline Pankhurst. Another thing to note about the cemetery – a conspiracy theory that there's a functioning time machine inside the tomb of socialite Hannah Courtoy. Her tomb was designed by an Egyptologist obsessed with time travel and it's said to be covered in hieroglyphics. Take a walk among the tombs and pretend you're in Paris.

—

Fulham Rd, London SW10 9UG
www.royalparks.org.uk/parks/brompton-cemetery
Opening times: 7am–7pm; winter 7am–4pm
Getting there: ⊖ West Brompton (District), Earl's Court (District/Piccadilly); ⤳ West Brompton

❀ CHELSEA PHYSIC GARDEN

Nestled by the River Thames, Chelsea Physic Garden is home to around 5,000 medicinal, herbal and edible plants. It's one of London's oldest gardens, and since 1673, has existed in four acres of land in London's Chelsea. It was originally founded to support apothecaries, tasked with finding cures for the myriad diseases that plagued historic London. Today, the sheltered garden, hemmed in by the centuries-old brick walls, creates a warm microclimate where a variety of plants can thrive. There are several must-sees, such as the world's most northerly outdoor grapefruit tree, and Britain's largest outdoor fruiting olive tree, but a real pleasure is walking around the ordered beds (arranged according to plant-classification), breathing in the cool air in the Victorian fernery, and exploring the garden of medicinal plants, which provides a fascinating look into the optimism of Western plant-based medical practice.

—

66 Royal Hospital Road, Chelsea, London SW3 4HS
www.chelseaphysicgarden.co.uk
Opening times: Monday–Friday, Sundays and Bank Holidays, 11am–6pm
Getting there: ⊖ Sloane Square

✿ MEANWHILE GARDENS

The narrow band of green alongside the Great Union Canal was only meant to be temporary – hence the original name 'meanwhile'. What was once a gravel-strewn stretch of land is now a tucked-away community garden in North Kensington, just minutes from bustling Ladbroke Grove and Portobello Road – with something for everyone. There's a free-to-use skate park at one end of the garden and a sensory hut to keep kids busy. But it's the other end of the gardens that will entice peace seekers to this private space: a discreet woodland area complete with ponds and wild flowers. Trees heavy with blossom hang over a spawn-filled pond which forms part of a peaceful wildlife area cultivated by Kensington and Chelsea Mind association, working with adults with mental-health issues. The gardens were restored in 2000, incorporating a gentle boardwalk that runs through the hedgerows and dense woodland.

—

156–158 Kensal Rd, London W10 5BN

Opening times: 24 hours

Getting there: ⊖ Westbourne Park (Hammersmith & City/Circle)

✿ ST DUNSTAN IN THE EAST

Catch this historic church on a sunny day and you'll feel as though you've stepped into Eden. Light slants through the empty arched windows highlighting the greens and yellows of the evergreen bushes that populate the old nave. After surviving for 300 years – damaged in the Great Fire of London, the church was restored and topped with a steeple designed by Sir Christopher Wren – it was badly bombed in the Blitz in 1941 and fell into ruin. Luckily for the people of London, rather than being redeveloped, in the 1960s it was transformed into a public garden with a lawn, trees and fountains. Keep your eyes peeled for the rare *drimys winteri* (winter's bark) in the lower garden, a plant whose leaves are heavy with vitamin C and which used to be widely eaten to keep scurvy at bay. It's a haven for lunchtime workers and those hunting out a slice of solitude from the city's hubbub.

—

St Dunstan's Hill, London EC3R 5DD

www.cityoflondon.gov.uk/things-to-do/green-spaces/city-gardens/visitor-information/Pages/St-Dunstan-in-the-East.aspx

Opening times: 8am–dusk

Getting there: ⊖ Monument (District/Circle)

❀ CAMLEY STREET NATURAL PARK

Camley Street Natural Park, a two-acre space in the heart of Kings Cross, is a vibrant wildlife spot in the centre of the city. Kids will love the small wildflower meadow and a nature-watching cabin to spy on visiting herons and kingfishers. The garden has expanded out into the river, with a peaceful floating platform designed by three Finnish architects who took inspiration from Scandinavia's coastline. The platform gives visitors a different perspective of the busy Regent's Canal in Kings Cross and kids can be seen on their hands and knees searching for tadpoles in the water. The new aquatic islands are ideal for attracting new amphibians to the area and frogs are already frequent visitors. Camley Street is currently being renovated and is due to open in spring 2019.

—

12 Camley Street, London N1C 4PW
Opening times: 10am–5pm, summer;
10am–4pm, winter
Getting there: ⊖ Kings Cross (Northern); ⇌ Kings Cross

❁ HIGHGATE CEMETERY

Divided into east and west sides, Highgate Cemetery is a beautiful north London garden cemetery. It's perhaps not surprising that its most famous resident, Karl Marx, is buried to the east. Highgate is an example of one of the world's finest Gothic cemeteries and there is just the right amount of peaceful, shady spots to contemplate one's mortality. The beautifully carved tombstones look more like works of art than headstones. Other than Marx, the cemetery houses many notable painters, creatives and musicians. Douglas Adams, author of *Hitchhiker's Guide to the Galaxy*, is buried here; while pop artist Patrick Caulfield's headstone, which spells out 'DEAD' in funky letters, is worth a gander. Poet Christina Rossetti is a resident of the west cemetery, while novelist George Eliot joins Marx in the east. An important part of London's history, Highgate Cemetery is a beautiful place to spend time in peace.

—

Swain's Lane, London N6 6PJ

www.highgatecemetery.org

Opening times: 10am–5pm (March to October);
10am–4pm (November to January)

East Cemetery admission: Adults £12; Children 8–17 £6

West Cemetery by guided tour only. Check website.

Getting there: ⊖ Highgate

🏵 NUNHEAD CEMETERY

The second largest, but possibly least celebrated of London's 'Magnificent Seven' cemeteries, Nunhead feels like a sprawling park rather than a cemetery. It's a wild place, perfect for scrambling walks, still dominated by the Gothic entrance gate and avenues of lime trees. The cemetery was designated a Site of Metropolitan Importance and like many of the cemeteries, it's a local nature reserve – tawny owls and woodpeckers are frequently spotted, so bring your binoculars. The tombs here range from cracked and broken to majestic. If you're after ruined Gothic chic check out the Nunhead Cemetery Chapel, destroyed by an arson attack in the 1970s but still used today to host concerts and readings. For a truly spectacular sight climb the hill on the western side of the cemetery and peer through the specially trimmed trees to view St Paul's Cathedral.

—

Linden Grove, London SE15 3LP
www.fonc.org.uk
Opening times: 8:30am–7pm
Getting there: ⇌ Nunhead

❀ SEXBY GARDEN

Hidden deep within Peckham Rye Park is Sexby Garden, sometimes called the Old English Garden. Laid out in period style, it has ornamental flower beds and a symmetrical design and at its centre is a gurgling fountain. In summer, the garden blooms with fragrant lavenders and herbs, making it feel like the secret kitchen garden of a royal palace rather than a public park. The park and common were designated for public use after industrialisation caused the population to boom in south London in the late 1880s. The four pagodas – added in the 1930s – are a nice touch, providing shade for picnicking families and shelter from sudden showers.

—

Peckham Rye Park, London SE15 3UA
www.peckhamryepark.org
Opening times: 7:30am–9pm
Getting there: ⇌ Peckham Rye

❀ ST ETHELBURGA'S

St Ethelburga's is an elegant seventeenth-century Christopher Wren-designed church in the heart of the City of London. It survived the Great Fire and the Blitz only to be devastated by an IRA bomb, then reopened as a 'maker of peacemakers'. The central courtyard is home to a peaceful walled garden, at the centre of which is a large Bedouin-style tent. Woven from goats hair, it has seating for 25. It also features memorials to those killed in recent and past London terror attacks.

—

78 Bishopsgate, London EC2N 4AG
www.stethelburgas.org
Opening times: First and third Monday, 11am–3pm
Getting there: ⊖ Liverpool Street (Central/Circle/District/Hammersmith & City/Metropolitan);
🚆 Liverpool Street

🌸 CROSSBONES GARDEN

Crossbones Garden is a quiet memorial park in the heart of Southwark, just minutes from The Globe theatre. It would be an unassuming little square if it weren't for the wall of flowers, ribbons and notes decorating one side of an iron gate. Monthly vigils are held in the park celebrating and mourning the lives of the 15,000 bodies believed to have been buried there since medieval times, mostly prostitutes, their bodies carelessly tossed into the unconsecrated land. Their bodies were gold mines for the grave robbers who would come and steal bodies to sell to doctors and scientists. Today, it's a lovely space to sit in and contemplate London's fast-changing fortunes and its layers of history.

—

Union Street, London SE1 1SD
www.crossbones.org.uk
Opening times: 12pm–3pm
Getting there: ⊖ Southwark (Jubilee), Borough (Northern/Jubilee)

✿ POSTMAN'S PARK

Thomas Griffin: died in a boiler explosion at a Battersea sugar refinery and was fatally scalded in returning to search for his friend. His is just one of the names on the Memorial to Heroic Self Sacrifice in Postman's Park, designed by artist George Frederic Watts to celebrate the lives of ordinary people who saved others from harm. The park, so-called because of its popularity with nearby General Post Office workers, has been immortalised in film. In *Closer*, Natalie Portman's character borrows the name Alice Ayres from one of the plaques. This shady space, moments from Aldersgate Street, is also home to several unusual species of plant – including banana and *davidia involucrata*, more commonly known as the Dove Tree.

—

St Martin's Le-Grand, London EC1A

www.cityoflondon.gov.uk/things-to-do/green-spaces/city-gardens/visitor-information/Pages/Postman's-Park.aspx

Opening times: 8am–5pm

Getting there: ⊖ St. Paul's (Central)

❀ JAPANESE ROOF GARDEN, SOAS

Look up in the heart of Bloomsbury and you might spot tendrils of wisteria creeping out over the roof of the Brunei Gallery, located in SOAS (the School of Oriental and African Studies). The roof garden is a homage to all things rocked and raked. *Karesansui*-raked gravel is the garden's highlight, while different rocks – granite, basalt and sandstone – provide a meditative atmosphere in which to contemplate life above the rooftops in this corner of central London. There is minimal planting here (in keeping with traditional Japanese rockeries and gardens) and Kanji symbols are engraved on stones around the gardens, while intricate spirals are raked into the *Ginshanada* gravel. The garden is dedicated to the concept of forgiveness, and it's a chilled place, perfect for taking a moment to breathe and let the stresses of your day drift away.

—

SOAS, University of London, Thornhaugh St, Russell Square, London WC1H 0XG
www.soas.ac.uk/soas-life/roofgarden
Opening times: Tuesday–Saturday, 10:30am–5pm
Getting there: ⊖ Goodge Street (Northern)

✿ TOWER HAMLETS CEMETERY PARK

Tower Hamlets is one of London's 'Magnificent
Seven' garden cemeteries, built in 1841. In
addition to Tower Hamlets, the cemeteries
include Highgate, Abney, Nunhead, Kensal Green,
Brompton and West Norwood. One of the
largest and most prominent graves belongs to
Joseph Westwood, who is buried under a 30-foot
spire. A factory owner, he went on to found the
football team that would eventually become
West Ham United. As well as exploring the
sometimes beautiful gravestones, follow paths
that wend their way past wildflower meadows
and through 10 hectares of lush woodlands during
your visit. Detour to the Scrapyard meadows,
which used to house old used car junkyards,
now transformed into a wildlife sanctuary. The
meadow is a site of Metropolitan Importance
for Nature Conservation: there are five wildlife
ponds and despite the highly acidic soil, beetles,
woodpeckers, foxes and tens of butterfly species
have made this park their home. Festivals, nature
days and walks take place here.

—

Southern Grove, London E3 4PX
www.fothcp.org
Opening times: 24 hours
Getting there: ⊖ Mile End (Central)

❀ CRYSTAL GROTTO, PAINSHILL

Painshill is a large private park, but it's also one of southern England's most beautiful landscaped gardens. Inside the park is a pink-stone Crystal Grotto which stands on the edge of the park's 14-acre lake – a Russian princess once described it as the 'sun penetrating through specially contrived cracks'. It's crammed with different crystals, attached to the walls and vault 'like icicles'. The grotto is a naturalistic cave covered in fake stalactites, rocks and glittering crystals. The gardens are a wonderful place to explore other Gothic structures, tramp through woodlands and watch herons dive for fish in the lakes. The whole park is a stunning example of eighteenth-century landscape gardening. It has hosted guests from Thomas Jefferson through to John Adams.

—

Portsmouth Road, Cobham, Surrey KT11 1JE0
Opening times: 11am–3pm (weekends only); Tickets: £8
Getting there: ⇌ Cobham & Stoke d'Abernon,
Walton-on-Thames, Weybridge

🌸 ST MARY ALDERMANBURY GARDENS

A bust of the Bard looks out approvingly over St Mary Aldermanbury Gardens on Love Lane, near Guildhall, a tiny pocket of green next to the City of London police headquarters. The church was bombed during the Second World War and the ruins shipped to Fulton, Missouri, where the rebuilt church now stands as a memorial to Churchill's 1946 Iron Curtain speech. The tiny green space in London acts as a memorial, too: actors Henry Condell and John Hemmings, who collected Shakespeare's works into the first folio in 1616, are both buried in the churchyard. The stone pillars that once supported the church remain as stumps, overgrown with weeds and grass – existing as a memory to the damage done to London by aerial bombardments. Now a pleasant lunch spot for off-duty police and lawyers working nearby, it is tranquillity in the midst of the City's chaos.

—

Love Lane, London EC2V
www.cityoflondon.gov.uk/things-to-do/green-spaces/
city-gardens/visitor-information/Pages/default.aspx
Opening times: 24 hours
Getting there: ⊖ Bank (Central/Northern/Waterloo & City/DLR), St Pauls (Central)

❀ RED CROSS GARDEN

Just off South Bank, the award-winning Red Cross Garden was designed by social reformer and co-founder of the National Trust, Octavia Hill, to be 'an open air sitting room for the tired people of Southwark'. Today, more often than not, it's full of tourists or workers munching their lunch. The pretty garden was built as a social housing experiment in the 1880s – Hill made it her mission to improve poor people's housing in London. The Shard dominates the skyline, but the greys and silvers of the surrounding office buildings and roads are softened by bushy ornamental grasses. The bandstand is still active – it plays host to occasional poetry and musical performances. As well as wide gravel paths and plenty of places to sit, there's also a rather large pond surrounded by wafting reeds and the occasional bird splashing around to cool down.

—

50 Redcross Way, London SE1 1HA
www.bost.org.uk/open-places/red-cross-garden
Opening times: Monday–Friday, 9am–5pm
Getting there: ⊖ Southwark (Jubilee), London Bridge (Jubilee/Northern)

❀ ST BOTOLPH WITHOUT BISHOPSGATE

The garden at St Botolph Without Bishopsgate is a verdant slither of peace surrounding a twelfth-century ornate church, damaged during a 1993 IRA attack. Look carefully around the churchyard and you'll notice a stone cross mounted on an octagonal plinth, under the stained-glass window, thought to be London's first ever First World War memorial – it was erected in 1916, during the war. There are plenty of other interesting facts about this church and lands – poet John Keats was baptised in the present font in 1795 and the adjoining tennis court is built on consecrated land, making it London's only holy sports pitch. It's still an active church, so even during the weekend, when much of the City is still and silent, the congregation can be found spilling out of the doors and enjoying the green space in the centre of one of the densest parts of London.

Bishopgate, London EC2M 3TL
www.cityoflondon.gov.uk/things-to-do/green-spaces/
city-gardens/visitor-information/Pages/St-Boltoph-
without-Bishopsgate.aspx
Opening times: 24 hours
Getting there: ⊖ Liverpool Street (Circle/Central/
Hammersmith & City/Metropolitan); ⇌ Liverpool Street

✿ WEST NORWOOD CEMETERY

One of the 'Magnificent Seven' cemeteries, West Norwood Cemetery spans an impressive 40 acres of land (and is home to 42,000 graves) in this otherwise highly residential part of the city. As well as being the perfect place to let off steam and enjoy the south London outdoors, the cemetery is home to some fascinating tombs and curios. The cemetery has an interesting layout, which you'll notice almost immediately. Laid out on a hill, it was the first London cemetery that attempted to reduce disease in this way – raised ground was believed to prevent the spread of disease. It also had the added benefit that the dead would be closer to heaven in a London, Christian, version of the Mount of Olives. As you walk around the shady paths that criss-cross through the cemetery, bear in mind that a huge catacomb network exists beneath your feet, complete with a miniature railway to transport bodies to the crematorium.

—

Norwood Rd, West Norwood, London SE27 9JU
Opening hours: 8am–4pm
Getting there: ⇌ West Norwood

WILD LONDON

WILD LONDON

Celebrated for its theatre, nightlife and shopping,
London is also home to thousands of species of plant,
mollusc and mammal - all who co-exist in a beautiful
symbiotic relationship with the city. One of the world's
biggest cities, it's remarkable that London has so many
nature reserves and sites of special scientific interest.
Most of the city's wild hot spots are managed by
the London Wildlife Trust, which looks after and
protects 41 spaces, from bogs to woodland, neighbourhood
gardens to wetlands. In this section, we include parks
that have dedicated wildflower gardens, woods that
have been allowed to grow outwards and upwards, and
scrubland, where deer and other mammals are allowed
to rut and roam free.

🌼 BUSHY PARK

North of Hampton Court, Bushy Park is packed full of things to explore on a sunny day, including ornate waterways, a Princess Diana memorial and a mile-long avenue of chestnut trees designed by Christopher Wren. The name 'Bushy' came from the old English word *bysce,* meaning 'thickly wooded'. The Waterhouse Woodland Garden is a woodland walk. Built in 1925, it weaves its way between two plantations and a sparkling glade of silver birch trees. Detour to the Pheasantry Welcome Café which serves up cake (freshly baked onsite) and tea in a gleaming new visitor centre in the heart of the woodland gardens. The Water Gardens area is well worth a mosey, too – these pools were built in 1710 by the Earl of Halifax but have since had other uses, such as acting as swimming pools for poor boys from the East End with respiratory problems. Today, the water gardens are made up of canals, cascades and channels – just the perfect place to hang out by on a scorching summer day.

—

Hampton Court Rd, Hampton TW12 2EJ
www.royalparks.org.uk/parks/bushy-park
Opening times: 24 hours (pedestrians);
6:30am–7:45pm (vehicles)
Getting there: ⇌ Teddington, Hampton Wick, Hampton Court

✿ HAMPSTEAD HEATH

One of London's most popular outdoor spaces, Hampstead Heath means many things to different people. For groups of friends, it's picnics and popping Prosecco corks; for couples, it means holding hands overlooking London's skyline at dusk; and for families, there are wild woods and lots of grass to play in. In summer, live music from the bandstands, children's parties and the screams of people throwing themselves into the famous cold bathing ponds or Lido pierce the air. In winter, it's great for a bracing walk before lunch in a nearby pub or café. The 320 hectares form a haven for wildlife: a quarter of all British species of spider have been found on the Heath and grass snakes have also been spotted during warm, quiet early mornings. Muntjac deer are occasionally seen leaping over fallen trunks, skirting into the woods, while gadwells and fieldfares can be found among the 180 bird species. Just four miles from central London, Hampstead has plenty of woodland pockets to get lost in, even in the height of summer.

—

Opening time: 24 hours
Getting there: ⊖ Highgate (Northern), Hampstead (Northern)

❀ STAVE HILL ECOLOGICAL PARK

After London's former docklands were transformed in the 1980s, Stave Hill was created with the waste from the site. Over time, it has developed into 5.2 acres of park overlooking Russia Wood (named after the dock which used to see delivery of goods from Russia). As well as woodland, the ecological park has been carefully maintained to conserve the large variety of flora and fauna found there. Birdwatchers can spot the usual blue tits, robins and blackbirds, while the odd kingfisher and parakeet can be seen fluttering among the trees. A sculpture by Michael Rizzello displays a map of the old dockyards cast in a bronze relief. When it rains, the channels of the map fill with water so they look like little rivers on top of the stone pillar.

—

Timber Pond Rd, London SE16 6AX
Opening times: 24 hours
Getting there: ⇌ Surrey Quays

✿ WOODBERRY WETLANDS

As the sun sets over Woodberry Wetlands the lakes glow orange, reflecting the burning sky. You'd be forgiven for thinking you were standing on a boardwalk in Cornwall, listening to the whisper of reed beds blowing in the sea breeze. Instead, you're in Hackney, sandwiched between Finsbury Park and Haringey Warehouse District. Today, the Wetlands are a real draw for wildlife lovers – shovelers, gadwalls (both ducks), bitterns (herons) and reed warblers fill the air with birdsong, while noctule and pipistrelle bats make their appearance as dusk falls. The site is spread over 12 hectares of land, threaded together by a wide and stable boardwalk, which runs across and between the two bodies of water. The Coal House Café provides refreshments, serving freshly roasted coffee and other necessities for a bracing walk around the water. Like the rest of the Wetlands, the juxtaposition between high-rise city living and the Norfolk Broads-style channels is remarkable. And, just for one second, watching coots build a nest on the banks, it can feel like a sliver of paradise in London.

—

Lordship Road, London N16 5HQ
Opening times: 9am–4:30pm every day (summer); 9am–4pm (winter)
Getting there: ⊖ Finsbury Park (Piccadilly, Victoria); ⇌ Finsbury Park

✿ CENTRE FOR WILDLIFE GARDENING

After years lying derelict, this brownfield site in Peckham Rye was transformed by the London Wildlife Trust into an award-winning urban oasis. The park is split into a series of microhabitats: a woodland copse, wildflower meadow (spot borage and cowslips), herb garden and four ponds. Sunflowers beam from raised beds and poppies wink red and black in the breeze. With such bio-diversity, you'll often find youth groups turning over stones in search of stag beetles, or locals enjoying the sun trap, listening to the goldfinches singing on the trees above. Paved pathways make the park accessible to wheelchairs and buggies. It's a glorious, fragrant space, made even sweeter by the stall selling honey produced by the centre's own bees.

—

28 Marsden Rd, London SE15 4EE

www.wildlondon.org.uk/reserves/centre-for-wildlife-gardening

Opening times: Thursday–Sunday, 10:30am–4pm

Getting there: ⇌ East Dulwich, Peckham Rye

✿ WALTHAMSTOW WETLANDS

On a clear day, the view from the top of the renovated pump house is spectacular – think handdug nineteenth-century reservoirs, avenues of poplars and rocky islands. Sandwiched between Tottenham and the Lea Valley and opened in October 2017, the Walthamstow Wetlands are Europe's largest urban wetlands with 13 miles of footpaths,10 reservoirs and 8 rocky islands populated with Europe's largest heronry. Their nests are massive, dominating the spindly trees which look like they're struggling to hold up their weight. The paths are flat and firm, making it easy to pace out the miles in such an idyllic location. For families, the building that once housed a steam pump engine has a café and kid-friendly exhibitions about local wildlife. It's a wetlands area that has stayed true to its roots and sensitive to its surroundings, while providing a welcome breathing space just 15 minutes by tube from the city's centre.

----

2 Forest Road, London N17 9NH

www.walthamstowwetlands.com

Opening times: 9:30am–5pm

Getting there: ⊖ Tottenham Hale (Victoria), Blackhorse Road (Victoria); ⇌ Blackhorse Road

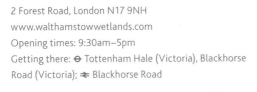

✿ EPPING FOREST

Gnarled beech trees and rough roots mark the transition from city to wild space. As London's largest open space, its 2,400-hectare sprawl allows Londoners to fish, camp and horseride just 30 minutes from central London. There is much to enjoy in Epping Forest's natural beauty – head there on a clear day in winter before the early morning mists have started to rise and walk to Barn Hoppitt, an ancient pollard wood with trees more than 500 years old. Try the short hike from High Beech up to Ambresbury Bank Iron Age Hill Fort, while keeping your eyes peeled for fallow deer, kept at Epping Forest Sanctuary, while buzzards, kestrels and hobby (falcons) fly overhead. The wood is a mountain-bikers paradise and there are plenty of trails to churn up mud. A decent cycle-hire outfit also rents out mountain bikes from around £20 for two hours: definitely a speedier way of getting off-track.

———

www.visiteppingforest.org
Getting there: ⊖ you can access the forest from various stops on the Central line, including Chigwell, Theydon Bois and Epping; ⇌ Epping

✿ LONDON WETLAND CENTRE

On a weekend morning, mist hangs on the glassy ponds and lakes of the London Wetland Centre in Barnes. A coot clucks its way out of the reeds, chased by a moorhen defending its nest. At quieter times you might see an otter splashing out of its holt, while kingfishers, great crested grebes and herons can all be spotted perching on the water's banks. Ring-necked parakeets, with their startling red beaks and green feathers, occasionally make an appearance alongside coscoroba swans and northern lapwings. There are tall bird hides to climb up into and watch the various wildlife. The centre is made up of four disused reservoirs, but there's little trace of the area's more functional past. There's a large visitor centre crammed with information, which also doubles up as a part-time light-filled wedding venue. The centre runs tours around the wetlands especially for kids to get a feel of the countryside.

—

Queen Elizabeth's Walk, Barnes, SW13 9WT
www.wwt.org.uk/wetland-centres/london
Opening times: 9:30am–5:30pm
Getting there: ⊖ Hammersmith (Piccadilly/District/Circle); ⇌ Barnes

❀ WILDERNESS ISLAND

This remarkable patch of wild space where two rivers meet is like *Swallows and Amazons'* Wild Cat Island, but in London. The designated Site of Special Scientific Interest sprawls between the River Wandle and the River Wrythe in south London and is managed by the London Wildlife Trust. Woodpeckers, grebes and kingfishers nest on the island, and visitors must arrive on foot to avoid disturbing the wildlife. The island is spotted with ponds that were once used by nearby Shepley House to keep carp as food for the household. Today they're populated with sticklebacks and stubby chub fish, while sparrowhawks circle overhead looking for dinner. It's a rich eco-system, all in one place, and you can explore the island properly using the nature trail. Enter the trail through a kissing gate at Mill Lane and Strawberry Lane in Carshalton.

—

Mill Lane, London SM5 2NH
www.wildlondon.org.uk/reserves/wilderness-island
Opening times: 24 hours
Getting there: ≋ Carshalton

❀ GREENWICH PENINSULA ECOLOGY PARK

Greenwich Peninsula Ecology Park is 4 acres of freshwater habitat, a wild space, overgrown with brambles, hawthorn and grasses that have been allowed to take root and thrive, all a hop and a skip from Greenwich in south London. It has two lakes, marshland, a small woodland and a meadow. A shingle beach lines the shore which provides a sloping shallow water for dragonflies, frogs and other amphibious creatures. Locals have recently spotted bats in nearby trees, a sign that the park is ticking boxes when it comes to creating environmental harmony. It is a tranquil, beautiful spot to take a walk and watch the birds and wildlife.

—

Thames Path, John Harrison Way, London SE10 0QZ
www.thelandtrust.org.uk
Opening times: Wednesday–Sunday, 10am–5pm (spring/summer), Wednesday–Sunday, 10am–dusk (autumn/winter)
Getting there: ⊖ North Greenwich (Jubilee);
⇌ Surrey Quays

✿ QUEEN'S WOOD

This thick, wonderful woodland is in London's Zone 2, just a short walk from Highgate Underground Station. Spindly hornbeam and ancient oaks dominate the wood, while a few tall beeches have grown above the canopy, pushing the branches of mountain ash and field maple out of the way. Despite its dense canopy, the forest floor is diverse and teeming with life – seasoned foragers can find wood sorrel in distinctive clumps under trees and upright trumpets of bluebells abound. Queens Wood is linked up to Harringay by the 12–mile Harringay Pathway. Take care to keep to marked trail and paths because the wood is also home to the rare jewel beetle. It's a perfect place to explore equally in sun or on a rainy day when the thick layer of leaves catches the rain and keeps you dry amid all the tumbling greens and climbing ivy.

—

London N10 3LD
www.fqw.org.uk
Opening times: 24 hours
Getting there: ⊖ Highgate (Northern)

✿ WIMBLEDON'S FARM BOG

It's unusual to find peat bogs in London but they're a crucial habitat for British wildlife. Bogs used to cover seven per cent of UK land but their coverage is reducing as urban centres sprawl – celebrate their presence and biological diversity while you still can. Wimbledon farm's peat bog can be found just north of the Iron Age fort remains – the bog, which looks like a swamp, was created when acidic water pooled on clay ground. Bad for those who forgot their boots, but brilliant for common lizards, wasp spiders and darters that make them their home. The bog is an old lady – it's been evolving for 6,000 years and as such, it's been named a Site of Scientific Special Interest and is protected by the London Wildlife Trust. Visitors are requested not to walk across or in the bog because it's a delicate ecosystem, and to use the footpaths that criss-cross Wimbledon Common. Dragonflies, damselflies, butterflies and bees love bogs – spend more than a few seconds by the bog on a hazy evening and you'll notice the hum of wildlife around the purple moorgrasses and bogbean.

—

Wimbledon Common, near Robin Hood Road, London SW19 5NR
Opening times: 24 hours
Getting there: ⇌ Wimbledon Station

WALKS

WALKS

Despite London's superlative public transport offerings, exploring the city on foot can help you appreciate it even more. Walking around the city helps you to understand the fabric of a city too, and understand the layers of history and change that have altered the way London has grown and Londoners live. Plus, walking around the city offers more than a simple stroll along the Thames (although this is an unmissable part of any visit to London). There are walks to suit any level of fitness, from relaxed strolls along the Thames' tributaries, to 78-mile loops around London's Green Belt. Best of all, many of the capital's walks feel rural, despite the proximity to the city's amenities. This means there's often a good pub nearby, and if you tire, there's normally a nearby bus stop or train station ready to whisk you back to the city. This section includes a mix of walks within the city, but also takes advantage of the fast train lines that spread out from the centre. So, what are you waiting for? Pull on your trainers, get outside and start walking. You'll hit something fabulous fast.

❀ EGHAM TO WINDSOR GREAT PARK

Just under an hour from London, few other close-to-the-capital walks offer up quite so much history as this 7.5-mile walk through Berkshire. On the walk from Egham to Windsor, there's something to look forward to around every corner – from Runnymede, where the Magna Carta was signed, to a large aircraft memorial statue. There's the John F. Kennedy memorial, inaugurated by Harold Macmillan in 1965, and then the white gates into Windsor Great Park loom. The walk wends its way through the park towards Windsor Castle and includes a final amble along the 2.5-mile Windsor Long Walk, which is headed up by a massive statue of King George III riding a horse. The walk is flat and easy to follow.

—

Distance: 7.5 miles
Terrain: Flat
Getting there: ⯮ Egham
Getting back: ⯮ Windsor and Eton Riverside

✿ LONDON'S OUTDOOR ORBITAL PATH

Covering 150 miles of London and split into 24 handy sections, the LOOP is the longest of London's big walks. It stands for the London Outer Orbital Path. It's the walker's version of the M25 and takes you around the city, threading through beautiful green spaces such as Hainault Country Park (once a royal hunting ground and now crammed with a lake, petting zoo and acres of ancient woodland) and Farthing Down. A sweeping 95 hectares of chalky grassland located within the Green Belt area, Farthing Down has a warren of walks and woodland paths all within easy reach of central London. The LOOP paths are easy to spot and follow – simply keep your eyes peeled for white discs with a blue kestrel on them.

—

Distance: Depends on the walk. See site.

Terrain: Mostly flat

Getting there: See site

www.tfl.gov.uk/modes/walking/loop-walk

✿ REGENT'S CANAL WALK

The Regent's Canal Walk showcases London in all its glory, starting in the basin behind Paddington Station and taking about half a day to complete at medium pace. The first section threads from Paddington to Regent's Park where pristine narrowboaters line up amid tiny gardens. It's likely you'll fall in love with the idea of living on a boat here. The path passes past London Zoo, with its aviaries on the left: spot brightly plumed birds and listen out for the roar of big cats. It then follows the canal past Kings Cross and into east London, passing busy Broadway Market and Victoria Park. It ends in Limehouse Basin, dominated by shiny metal-fronted, water-facing cafés and restaurants.

Distance: 8.5 miles
Terrain: Firm and accessible
Getting there: ⊖/≷ Paddington (District/Circle)
Getting back: ≷ Limehouse DLR

❀ THE THAMES PATH

As the Thames flows from source to estuary, from the Cotswolds to the sea, a path runs alongside it. The Thames Path is split into different sections, which make this 79-mile part of it manageable. The London section of the walk kicks off on the north bank at Hampton Court and follows the river all the way to the River Darent and the eastern marshes as the river begins to slow and make its way to the sea. This walk packs in some of London's most important sights including the Palace of Westminster, Hampton Court Palace, Syon House, a glimpse into a corner of Kew Gardens, and Chelsea's wonderful pink and green Albert Bridge. Apart from a few bridge crossings between the north and south bank, the walk simply follows the river and has signs with a white acorn on a blue disk, the Thames Path National Trail Symbol.

—

Distance: 79 miles

Terrain: Mostly flat

Getting there: ⇌ Hampton Court

Getting back: ⇌ Slade Green

www.tfl.gov.uk/modes/walking/thames-path

🌸 WIMBLEDON STATION TO RICHMOND STATION

If you're ever short of time (and energy) but crave a quick blast in the open air, consider this handy walk from Wimbledon Train station to Richmond. It crams plenty in a short distance, passing across Wimbledon Common before dipping down into some lovely deep beech woods. The walk threads through the trees, along a gurgling stream and into Richmond Park. At the park gates choose your poison – you can rent a bike, have a picnic, or easily spend a few hours hiking around the park, which in winter you may find blanketed in thick white mist. Spot red and fallow deer which have freely roamed Richmond Park since 1637; they play an important role in park maintenance, eating seedlings, leaves and twigs from the ground. Drop back down into Richmond town centre, following one of the prettiest parts of the Thames back towards the station.

—

Distance: 5 miles

Terrain: Some hills, firm underfoot

Getting there: ⊖ Wimbledon (District); ⇌ Wimbledon

Getting back: ⊖ Richmond (District); ⇌ Richmond

✿ CAPITAL RING WALK

This 78-mile walk passes through nature reserves, parks and urban woodlands hills and is divided into 15 sections. Highlights include Beckenham Place Park, the Walthamstow Wetlands and the beautiful Abney Park cemetery, one of the 'Magnificent Seven'. If you were to visit London and only did this walk, you'd leave feeling like the capital was an urban oasis of green. While the parks and woodlands hide the chaotic city, often just a few hundred metres away, the walk links up important parts of the city – like Hackney and Richmond. It's a satisfying walk and one that could be done over a couple of summer weekends, or schlepped all in one go over a week, depending on your speed. Apart from Highgate and Crystal Palace, the walk is on firm ground and mostly flat. It can be started, stopped and resumed at any point in its circle – just look for a white disk on a wooden post with a blue Big Ben logo on it.

—

Distance: 78 miles

Terrain: Firm and mostly flat

Getting there: See site

www.tfl.gov.uk/modes/walking/capital-ring

– includes route maps

🌼 THE GREEN CHAIN WALK

The Green Chain walk shines a spotlight on
London's less-explored south-east regions.
The walk stretches from the River Thames at
Thamesmead down to deepest Nunhead, a 50-
mile collection of paths passing castles, abbeys
and galleries. Split into 11 easy-to-walk sections,
the Green Chain links up south London's strips of
woodland and parks. Highlights include Lesnes
Abbey in Abbey Wood, dating from 1178 and
destroyed by Henry VIII during the dissolution
of the monasteries, and Oxleas meadows, one of
the few remaining strips of ancient woodlands
in the south-east. Enjoy south-east London's
beauty, quietly, squelching across Plumstead
Common, through Bostall Woods and into the
Green Flag-winning Shepherdleas Wood. The walk
is clearly signposted – in woods and parks, paths
are denoted with yellow posts, while along roads
the letters G–C, or Green Chain, point you in the
right direction.

—

Distance: 50 miles
Terrain: Firm and mostly flat
Getting there: There are 11 different sections of this
walk, so use the handy TfL guide to decide which leg
of the walk you want to do.
www.tfl.gov.uk/modes/walking/green-chain-walk

🏵 THE WANDLE TRAIL: MORDEN TO WANDSWORTH

The Wandle Trail is a well-marked path alongside south London's River Wandle, which stretches for 5.7 miles through Wandsworth town centre and towards the Thames. The walk begins in Morden Hall Park and continues along the clearly marked Wetlands Boardwalk. The Wandle once powered 90 mills but most are now defunct, replaced by light industry and warehouses along its banks. The path clearly follows the river, past the Merton Abbey Mills complex where William Morris operated a textile mill in the 1880s. Eared-willow and broad-bodied chaser dragonflies hover over the pools of water after heavy rains – frogs, toads and newts make the most of the park's wetlands. The walk finishes by crossing into Wandsworth town and passes through the Young's Brewery Complex before joining the River Thames.

—

Distance: 5.7 miles
Terrain: Easy, flat, paved
Getting there: ⊖ Morden (Northern)
Getting home: ⇌ Wandsworth

✿ RIVER VER

This trail, between Harpenden and St Albans, follows the River Ver through the flat expanses of Hertfordshire countryside. Harpenden and St Albans are well in the commuter belt, which means there are frequent fast trains right into central London. This walk is packed full of historical sites, from the Roman Theatre of Verulamium to the magnificent and ancient St Albans Cathedral. The walk follows part of the Nicky Line, a disused railway line, fringed with hawthorn and blackberries, while another section of the path takes you past the attractive Redbournbury Mill, which has ground flour for hundreds of years. A stall outside occasionally sells fresh bread to visitors. Those looking for a good pint should detour to Ye Olde Fighting Cocks pub which dates from the sixteenth century and is believed to be the oldest pub in England.

—

Distance: 8.7 miles
Terrain: Flat
Getting there: ⇌ Harpenden
Getting home: ⇌ St Albans

✿ CHALFONT AND LATIMER TO KINGS LANGLEY

For some Londoners, the idea you can take a tube right out into the countryside requires some getting used to. Take the Metropolitan Line out to Zone 8's Chalfont and Latimer Station. From here, it's a brief walk to a path that plunges through a copse of beech trees and into the Chess Valley, which on sunny days looks like the sort of 1950s Enid Blyton-esque landscape. This walk follows the well-signposted Chess Valley walk, climbing gently along the Chess Valley Trail which leads you down a lovely lane towards the 22-chimneyed Chenies Manor, frequently seen in *Midsomer Murders*. The well-marked trail signposts towards Sarrat Church, which takes you across several muddy-after-rain fields towards the tower of the twelfth-century building where John le Carré set his fictional spy training academy in his Cold War novels. Stop off for a decent lunch at the Cricketers Pub, and end the walk by passing Chipperfield Common, past Bronze Age burial mounds, and along a dry valley towards Kings Langley.

—

Duration: 8.75 miles
Terrain: Some hills, may be muddy after rain
Getting there: ⊖ Chalfont and Latimer (Metropolitan)
Getting back: ⇝ Kings Langley to London Euston
(31 minutes)

✿ LEA VALLEY WALK: LIMEHOUSE BASIN TO TOTTENHAM HALE

An important navigational channel even in medieval times, this 7.5-mile section of the 50-mile walk runs through the greater Lee Valley Regional Park. The walk is a straightforward line – point your nose north from the Thames and you can hop off wherever you fancy en route. Along the walk you'll see the Olympic stadium on your right; the rest of the walk ambles through Hackney Wick, alongside the windswept and almost rural expanse of Hackney Marsh. Take a detour to peek at the heron nests in Walthamstow Wetlands (see Wild London/ page 93), or keep to the river, as it curves around its bulge, passing Warwick Reservoir to your right. Follow the river for another 500m until you arrive at Tottenham Hale tube station.

—

Distance: 7.5 miles

Terrain: Firm underfoot, accessible paths

Getting there: ⇌ Limehouse DLR

Getting home: ⊖ Tottenham Hale (Victoria)

www.visitleevalley.org.uk

🌸 PARKLAND WALK VIA HAMPSTEAD HEATH

The Parkland walk follows the old tracks of an abandoned railway line built in the 1860s that once ran between Finsbury Park and Alexandra Palace. It wends its way past busy Finsbury Park to peaceful Highgate and winds through steep-sided woodland towards Highgate Village, where the path veers off towards the main road. A lovely alternative, especially during a humid summer, is to cut up towards Hampstead Heath through Highgate Village. Grab a bite from the Highgate Pantry and head through Highgate Village Green, dropping down Highgate Hill and along Merton Lane onto Hampstead Heath. Go for a dip in one of the bathing ponds: time your visit well, early in the morning or late evening, and you might just have one all to yourself. It's a great walk for those with buggies as it's accessible the whole way.

—

Distance: 4 miles
Terrain: Sturdy terrain, some gradual hills
Getting there: ⊖ Finsbury Park (Victoria)
Getting away: ⊖ Kentish Town (Northern)

✿ THE LOW LINE

Better Bankside has created a walk they've called the Low Line, which runs along the old viaduct in a fascinating and rapidly evolving part of London. Union Street is packed with art galleries, great restaurants and independent theatres, while there are prime coffee roasters and brunch spots around every other corner. The Globe theatre, the redevelopment of Borough Market and the Tate Modern have made this a buzzing place to visit – and now it's the turn of the old viaduct to shine. Linking London Bridge with Elephant and Castle, The Low Line showcases spaces like the popping

Flat Iron Yard and the Union Yard Arches, which houses Bala Baya, a phenomenal Tel Aviv-focused restaurant, the Spanish-language Cervantes Theatre and the award-winning Union Theatre. It's a lovely little walk that showcases a less polished part of London, but that's what makes following this south London beast so interesting.

—

Distance: 3 miles
Terrain: Flat, accessible
Getting there: ⊖ London Bridge (Northern/Jubilee)
Getting away: ⊖ Elephant and Castle (Northern/Bakerloo)
www.betterbankside.co.uk/buf/the-low-line

BIKES

BIKES

Cycling is one of the best ways to see London. Thanks
to significant investment in cycling infrastructure,
it's getting easier to get from A to B by bike. Many
roads have bike lanes separated with a concrete hump
from the traffic, while painted blue cycle superhighways
allow cyclists to zip across the capital. Be alert: try
to avoid squeezing down the left-hand side of a bus or
lorry, staying well clear altogether if it's turning,
and keep your eyes peeled for taxis and buses that pull
in frequently. Note that you can't take bikes on buses or
the tube, but they should be fine to go on mainline train
services outside of rush-hour. London's a great city to
explore on two wheels – it's often the quickest way so
strap a helmet on and enjoy the ride.

❀ BROCKWELL PARK TO DULWICH

After a quick dip in Brockwell Lido, or a swift coffee at the formidable Lido Café, hop on your steed and exit the park by the Bullfinch Brewery. The roads between Herne Hill and Dulwich are bordered by white picket fences and feel more English village than south London. The ride between the two parks shouldn't take longer than 25 minutes, so if you want to, extend your ride with a loop around Dulwich Park. Detour to the American rose gardens to revel in the fragrant flowers, or kick back and have an ice cream by the boating pond if it's a real scorcher of a day. On a chillier or more overcast day, stop off in the brilliant Dulwich Picture Gallery, with its collection of early twentieth-century paintings, for a browse and refuel before riding back towards Herne Hill. This is a perfect family bike ride to get kids acclimatised to cycling on London's backstreets.

—

Distance: 2 miles one way, 4 miles round-trip
Terrain: Gentle
Getting there: ⇌ Herne Hill

✿ RAINHAM MARSHES

Part of the Thames Estuary, Rainham Marshes' 411 hectares of low-lying land is managed by the RSPB and is home to plenty of birds, insects and the rare water vole. Waders and lapwings call as you peddle your bike around the marshes. If you don't have a bike, you can rent one at the visitor centre for £10 for a full day (£8 for members), then follow one of the suggested cycling routes. The Reserve Loop is 5.3 miles long and runs along the wall of the estuary. Keep your eyes peeled for seals and listen out for the mating calls of marsh frogs. A much longer route is the Ingrebourne Hill Loop, a 12.4 mile ride which goes more off-road than the Reserve Loops and takes in tranquil ponds, woodland and a number of hills through Hornchurch Country Park, a more strenuous cycle. There's also a 1.2 mile-mountain-biking section, so you can pump up your adrenaline in the middle of the 12.4 mile circuit.

—

New Tank Hill Rd, Purfleet RM19 1SZ
Distance: Reserve Loop: 5.3 miles; Ingrebourne Hill Loop: 12.4 miles
Terrain: Reserve Loop, easy/flat; Ingrebourne Hill Loop: challenging, hilly
Opening times: 9.30am–4.30pm
Getting there: ⇌ Purfleet
www.rspb.org.uk/reserves-and-events/reserves-a-z/rainham-marshes/

🌸 PEASLAKE, SURREY HILLS

Mountain bikers looking for the thrill of off-roading close to London will love biking in Peaslake. On either side of Peaslake village, which sits nestled in a valley between two thickly wooded hills, perfect trails stretch out in fingers on both sides. The trails around here can host about 1,000 bikers a week in the height of summer. The drizzly rains of winter bring their own obstacles and challenges to the paths for more experienced riders. Pine needle-soft paths deaden the sound of tyres through the woods, heightening the feeling of being alone in a massive biking playground. Recommended runs include Proper Bo, a route featuring slaloming and chunky logs to bike over, and Yoghurt Pots, so-called because the route is dominated with swampy bits so thick with mud there's a strong chance you'll end up coated.

—

Peaslake, Guildford GU5
Distance: See trails on site
Terrain: Challenging
Getting there: ⇌ Gomshall, via Dorking from London Waterloo
www.surreyhillsmtber.co.uk; for more information about the trails: http://hurtwoodtrails.co.uk

❀ VICTORIA PARK TO EPPING FOREST

There's no better way to ease into hipster-filled east London than by exploring it on two wheels. This ride covers a lot of ground, but there's enough en route to keep you interested. It's also a simple trail to follow – no getting off and checking map apps every minute. Victoria Park (see Parks/page 23) is a busy place to start a ride, and depending on the season, could be rammed with picnicking Londoners playing music and drinking craft beer on the grass. The ride leaves the park and joins the Hertford Union Canal straight out of the park, which then turns into the River Lea towpath. Follow this for 10 miles passing the Olympic Park on your right, shortly followed by the reservoirs in Ponders End before heading into peaceful Epping Forest.

—

Distance: 12 miles
Terrain: Gentle
Getting there: Cycle to Victoria Park
Getting away: ⇌ Chingford
www.visiteppingforest.org

✿ CRYSTAL PALACE TO NORTH DOWNS

A challenging, hilly bike ride, the route from Crystal Palace (see Parks/page 20) to the North Downs, a chalk ridge in south-east England, feels like a straight arrow into the countryside. The route is tough and long – at 30 miles this is a good afternoon's ride or, if you want to take it easy, a whole day at the weekend. The Corkscrew Lane ascent is one of the tougher parts of the ride – it's a real thigh-punisher. At the top there's a chance for a breather and to enjoy the view over south London as the road climbs through ancient woodland past expanses of farmland and vegetation. Cyclists are rewarded by a stunning view of the North Downs, which roll onwards until they join the South Downs and then on to the sea and the English Channel. The most enjoyable part of the ride is still to come – a dip down to the village of Westerham, where you can get up to 40mph speeding downhill on your bike.

—

Distance: 30 miles
Terrain: Challenging
Getting there/away: ⇌ Crystal Palace

🌸 PUTNEY TO HAMPTON COURT ALONG THE THAMES

Long, flat walks make brilliant cycle paths and this one, which passes the old Harrod's furniture storage building, through shaded woodland glens, and alongside river islands, or eyots as they're known on the Thames, is the best of the lot. Thanks to the river-hugging railway line, you can keep cycling until your legs hurt, and then pull your wheels onto the train at Hampton Court, Barnes or even as far as Walton-on-Thames. A good 12-mile ride brings you to cross the old packhorse bridge at Kingston and peddle past the locks at Teddington, where rowers speed along in narrow-bodied sculls. Cyclists share the path with pedestrians and dogs, so it's not a ride for speedsters. Instead, join the ambling families and relaxed walkers and drift from pub to coffee shop to ice-cream stand, as you weave your way along the easy-to-follow river path.

—

Distance: 12 miles
Terrain: Fairly even
Getting there: ⊖ Putney (District); ⇌ Putney
Getting away: ⇌ Hampton Court, Barnes, Walton-on-Thames

✿ WIMBLEDON TO WALTON-ON-THAMES

A ride that takes in rural London at its best, Wimbledon to Walton-on-Thames crosses commons, parks, riverbanks and woods. Go on a quiet Saturday or Sunday morning, just as the sun has risen above the tree line. During early summer, silvery slivers of light shine through the green canopy that covers part of the riverside path from Hampton Court to Walton-on-Thames, while in winter, the chill of the Thames keeps you on your toes along the water. The route passes through Richmond Park (see Parks/pages 24-25), following the uphill road to Pen Ponds Café for about 1km. There's a sign pointing towards the 'Isabella Plantation', the extensive woodland gardens. Follow this smooth tarmacked road towards pretty Ham Common, the second largest conservation area in the Borough of Richmond, gifted by Charles I to the people until 'the end of time'. Glimpse grand Hampton Court through the gold gates as you speed along the river path towards Walton-on-Thames.

—

Distance: 12 miles
Terrain: Gentle
Getting there: ⊖ Wimbledon (District); ⇌ Wimbledon
Getting away: ⇌ Walton-on-Thames

✿ HYDE PARK TO CHELSEA PHYSIC GARDEN

Although cycling across London can, at times, feel chaotic and stressful, the real beauty of this city is finding calm backstreets lined with trees and bike lanes. There are plenty of green areas across the city, where the traffic is lighter and you really feel as though you're getting a 'behind-the-scenes' version of the city. This ride from Hyde Park to Chelsea Physic Garden is short enough to clock under 30 minutes with the TfL cycle hire scheme. The route covers the park, passing the architecturally stunning Serpentine Galleries in Kensington Gardens, before dropping down towards the magnificent Royal Albert Hall and the Victoria and Albert Museum. The Physic Garden (see Secluded Places/page 59), at the end of your ride, is one of London's more beautiful 'secret' gardens so they're worth a peek. The oldest botanical gardens in London, it's also home to the largest fruit-giving olive tree in the country, an unexpected find in any corner of London.

—

Distance: 3.5 miles

Terrain: Gentle

Getting there: ⊖ Hyde Park (Piccadilly), Bayswater (Circle/District), Queensway (Central)

Getting away: ⊖ Sloane Square (Circle/District)

www.tfl.gov.uk/modes/cycling/santander-cycles

❀ SWINLEY FOREST BIKE TRAILS

Managed by the Windsor estate, Swinley Forest is nestled between Bracknell and Bagshot. With a thousand acres of Scottish pine trees and 24km of purpose-built mountain bike trails, there's a route for everyone. Less experienced cyclists, or those out of practice, should take the green trails and leave the blue trails for cyclists with basic off-roading abilities. The red trails provide a more hard-core biking experience, while the more advanced slopes promise hairpin bends, gravel path descents and plenty of single tracks summiting steep hills. Bikers and birdwatchers can spot nightjars and woodlarks as they cycle, and there's a slightly ethereal atmosphere as you pedal among the pines on a rainy, misty morning. You don't necessarily need a fat-tyred bike to enjoy all the trails and if you've been looking at getting into mountain biking for a while, this is the place to start.

—

Bracknell RG12 7QW

Opening times: 9am–4:30pm; Saturday, 9am–6pm

Distance: See trails

Terrain: See trails; varies according to experience

Getting there: ⇌ Bracknell from London Waterloo

www.swinleybikehub.com/trails

🌸 LEE VALLEY MOUNTAIN BIKE TRAIL

It's one thing gently pedalling along London's backstreets, and quite another gunning down a dirt track at 40mph, wind in hair, heart in mouth. Mountain biking is one of the most liberating activities you can do within the M25, and luckily, there's a wonderful mountain bike trail just by the Olympic Park. If you've never mountain-biked before, Lee Valley offers introductory sessions to get you used to cycling on the grit and gravel, while beginners courses go one step further and teach you to control your bike. Sign up to a family session to get the whole family on two wheels barrelling down tracks and across grit bridges. The bike trails offer five miles of courses and it's an urban centre – so don't come expecting fir trees and log trails balanced across roaring rivers. This is breeze block, concrete and gravel territory. Beginners will be encouraged to wear suitable padding and there's a good mix of gentler slopes and twisting, vertical challenges for more advanced riders.

—

Distance: See site

Terrain: Manmade

Getting there: ⊖ Stratford (Jubilee); ⇌ Stratford

www.visitleevalley.org.uk/en/content/cms/london2012/velo-park/mountain-biking

❀ THE TAMSIN TRAIL

Richmond Park (see Parks/pages 24-25) isn't just for deer and day ramblers; there's also a good 7.5-mile park route known as the Tamsin Trail, which uses its well-tarmacked roads and sweeping curves to guarantee a smooth ride. You'll be riding on a shared path with walkers, so be respectful. The path runs around Richmond Park and can be joined from any of the park's four gated entrances. There are some short climbs near the Kingston Gate and a slow incline near Pembroke Lodge, but really, this ride is pleasurable and relaxed, punctuated by dogwalkers and the almost rural expanse of the Isabella Plantation.

—

Distance: 7 miles
Terrain: Well-tarmacked roads and paths
Opening times: Pedestrian gates are open all year round; vehicle gates open at 7am– dusk (summer), 7:30am–dusk (winter)
Getting there: ⊖ Richmond (District); ⇌ Richmond

WATER

WATER

Nothing eases a stressed mind more than splashing around on a dusky summer's evening or gently paddling around on narrowboats and cruisers. Being on the river is a different experience: we become part of nature again, able to observe and absorb the habits of wildlife as we punt or chug along Regent's Canal or the Lea Valley. Many of London's parks and secluded spaces are connected in some way to water. This is a green city but also a water-abundant one. Birds watch, heads cocked, gliding along the calm water following the boats. Keep your eyes peeled for nesting coots, and the distinctive clicking of the red-beaked moorhens.

London is interlinked with canals and rivers, promising perfect conditions for novice watersports enthusiasts. Paddleboarding and kayaking are the most exposed you can be on the water, without actually being in it. The chilled river water laps over your toes as you push, steadily bobbing, waiting for the wake of a passing boat to subside. It's a novel way to explore the city, and one, with just a little forward planning, you can easily enjoy.

✿ ISLEWORTH AIT – KAYAKING ALONG THE THAMES

There are more than 80 islands in the River Thames, and Isleworth Ait is one of them. Located at the mouth of the River Crane, off Old Isleworth, it is accessible only by boat and with prior permission from the London Wildlife Trust. Although an undisturbed sanctuary for birds, insects and animals, there's no harm in kayaking around it and peering in at the overgrown crack willow, hawthorn bushes and bright marsh marigolds which come alive with the buzz of bees and dragonflies in midsummer. The rare German hairy snail and the two-lipped snail call the island home, prey to the kingfishers and herons that also live there. Bear in mind that access is very limited and preserving the wildlife is paramount. If you want to land, there are occasional public open days throughout the year which you can find on the London Wildlife Trust site.

—

London Borough of Hounslow, London TW7 6XH
Activity: Kayaking – kayaks available from
www.kayakinglondon.com
Distance: 2 miles
Getting there: ⊖ Richmond (District); ⇌ Richmond

✿ CANOEING THE LIMEHOUSE LOOP

With about 100km of waterways across London, there are plenty of places to get involved in the rhythmic paddle of kayaks gliding past old houseboats and coots' nests. One of the best is Limehouse Basin, a starting-point for a four-hour trip, in a two-seater canoe, around the surrounding canals. The canal loops in a square back to Limehouse Basin, where there are plenty of pubs and cafés to put your newly strengthened biceps into play. Rent your kayaks from Moo Canoes in Limehouse, which will kit you out with a life vest before you start your trip along Limehouse Cut towards Bromley-by-Bow. Drift through east London, past new housing developments, the canalside section of Victoria Park, and admire the view of the magnificent Olympic Stadium. If you want your food to reflect your time spent in the water, drag your boat out at the Forman's Smokery, a salmon smokehouse with big glass window vistas of the canal.

—

Limehouse Basin, 30 Pinnacle Way, London E14 7JZ
Activity: Canoeing – canoes available from Moo Canoes
www.moocanoes.com
Duration: 4 hours
Getting there: ⇌ Limehouse DLR

❀ PADDLEBOARDING THE GRAND UNION

Paddleboarding at Paddington Basin shows a totally different side to west London. The canal is far less choppy than the Thames, the water shallower and there are plenty of tourists to wave at as you flail and try not to fall in. London's canals all link up the Grand Union, running seamlessly into Regent's Canal. If you want to stay on the Grand Union a good two-hour route would be to paddle down to Little Venice, a wealthy area of London crammed with eighteenth- and nineteenth-century houses and blooming flower beds. Keep your eyes peeled for Rembrandt Gardens: to mark the 700th anniversary of the city of Amsterdam in 1975, this stretch of green – previously known as Warwick Avenue Garden – took receipt of 5,000 tulips and 500 hyacinths and planted them in ornamental flower beds. Paddleboarding sessions run all week but are subject to cancellation in bad weather.

—

Merchant Square, Paddington, London W2 1JZ
Activity: Paddleboarding – rent boards from Active360
www.active360.org
Duration: 1–2 hours
Getting there: ⊖ Paddington (Bakerloo/Circle/District);
⇌ Paddington

✿ REGENT'S CANAL TO HACKNEY

This is a fascinating part of London to drift down, packed with narrowboat dwellers, cats sunning themselves on boats and tourists ambling along the side of Regent's Canal. If you don't have your own kayak or inflatable boat, then there are several outfits that rent kayaks and canoes out to adventurous spirits. Starting at Paddington Basin and paddling east towards Camden Lock will give you a completely fresh perspective on London as you watch narrowboats sink and rise as they wait their turn to pass through the locks. The water is cleaner than ever before. A concerted effort is being made by the council to do frequent litter picks, and you'll spot coots, moorhens and heron living happily by the water as you paddle towards Victoria Park. If you don't have your own kayak, book a trip with London Kayak Tours and choose the lush green route running alongside London Zoo and Regent's Park. This route only goes as far as Camden and has an entry point at Prince Albert Road. Sessions last for 90 minutes.

—

Activity: Kayaking/canoeing – tours available from www.londonkayaktours.co.uk/sales
Duration: 1.5 hours
Getting there: ⊖ St John's Wood (Bakerloo)

❀ PADDLEBOARDING FROM KEW TO RICHMOND AND BACK

Paddleboarding down the Thames from the green-fringed banks of Kew towards Richmond is a beautiful route. Paddlers head towards Lot's Ait, a pretty island in the centre of the Thames, and then along the river's left bank to glimpse the stately Kew Palace. Further along, ring-necked parakeets screech from the tree tops, puffing up their green plumage as they hop from branch to branch. On a quiet day you may see sparrowhawks circling the river, preparing a swallow dive into the trees to catch smaller fowl . You'll likely pass sculling boats, their blades glancing off the water in rhythmic obedience, flying over the crest of the Thames' chop. They leave you far behind though, and you can plough on, enjoying the cool water lapping over your toes as you paddle towards Richmond. At the end of the route, paddleboarding outfits provide a return service, so you don't have to schlep all the way back upstream.

—

Distance: 3.2 miles
Activity: Paddleboarding – paddleboards are available from Active 360 www.active360.org, just under Kew Bridge
Duration: 2 hours
Getting there/back: ⇌ Kew Bridge

155

✿ LEE VALLEY WHITE WATER CENTRE

White water rafting can be whites-of-your-eyes level scary, but the fun sessions held at Lee Valley White Water Centre will ease you into navigating the rapids. Different levels of experience are catered for, from family sessions to getting wetsuited-and-booted with friends before barrelling down the Olympic-standard competition course. If you want to try things out without the big group, then you can rent a 'hot dog' – a kind off inflatable two-seater canoe which will roll you down the rapids closer to the action. The 300m Olympic Standard Competition Course has a drop of 5.5m from the start of the course to the end and promises to get your stomach churning throughout.

—

Station Road, Waltham Cross, Hertfordshire EN9 1AB
Activity: White water kayaking –
www.gowhitewater.co.uk
Duration: Varies
Opening times: 8am–6pm/8pm
Getting there: ⇌ Waltham Cross

✿ STAND UP PADDLEBOARDING ROUTES FROM TWICKENHAM

Stand Up Paddleboarding (SUP) on the Thames isn't all waves and wash – thanks to the curves and eyots in the river, there are calmer sections which are perfect for beginners to explore the Thames, while more proficient SUPers can take a board all the way down towards Hammersmith. The SUP routes from Twickenham though are glorious – and the least 'urban' routes available to paddle in London. Passing beautiful Marble Hill Park, famous Eel Pie Island (once home to rock music festivals and an alternative living commune), and the nature reserve of Ham Lands, it's easy to feel like you're deep in the countryside. Best of all, there are frequent train stations, so when you finish your dusk post-work paddle, you'll never be too far away from transport to zip you straight back into town and home.

—

Activity: Stand Up Paddleboarding
Duration: Varies
www.epicsup.org/coaching.html
Getting there: ⇌ Twickenham

✿ HAMPSTEAD HEATH PONDS

Hampstead Heath Ponds is the general term for a series of former reservoirs found in Hampstead and Highgate, fed by the clear, fresh waters from the River Fleet, the largest of London's subterranean rivers. They are places to de-stress before plunging back into city life, feeling invigorated. Here, people float among fellow swimmers: there's no racing or triathlon training. There are no barriers, no lanes, and no artificial constructs – just water, birds, mud, leaves and people who want to sink into nature. Kingfishers come to drink by the side of the pond and herons stand guard, keeping their beady eyes peeled for fish. New swimmers may be surprised by just how quickly they take to the cold water – even at the height of summer the pools' temperature rarely increases past 22 degrees. Kenwood Ladies Pond is more shaded than the men's or mixed ponds; while wonderful for privacy, this also means the water cools down quickly as soon as the sun begins to set. Swimmers must wear swimming costumes, and hand insulation gloves are recommended during cooler months.

——

Opening times: Depends on season; prices apply – check website

Getting there: ⊖ Highgate Tube (Northern), Hampstead (Northern); ⇌ Hampstead

www.cityoflondon.gov.uk/things-to-do/green-spaces/hampstead-heath/swimming/Pages/ponds-times-charges.aspx

✿ THE RIVER WEY

Just a few miles outside of Guildford is the Wey Navigation. Mud and sand ooze between toes on the river bed, which makes it perfect for a soft, gentle immersion into the cold water. A refreshing change from the chlorine-filled pool, rivers feel alive to swim in as cautious fish make themselves known, glancing past knees and elbows.

The River Wey has been swum in for ever – there are subtle entry points laid out along the water. One of the easiest places to clamber in is where the river gently slopes about a mile upstream of the old railway bridge. Look out for a few wooden stumps worn down by hands using them to haul themselves out of the water. Having a non-swimming companion to carry clothes and valuables is perfect for this stretch of the river, as instead of a quick dip, swimmers can extend their activity south towards Guildford, where half a mile downstream there's a wider sandy beach perfect for clambering out.

—

Getting there: Train to Guildford (Mainline from London); River Wey Footpath

✿ BROCKWELL LIDO

London has a surprising number of outside pools. Plunging into cold water solves many problems, whether you overdid it the night before or you're feeling achy after exercise. Cold water causes an adrenaline spike, cancelling out head fuzziness and leaving you fit and fighting for the day ahead. Get to Brockwell Lido at day break when slivers of golden sun are glancing off the surface of the water and you'll feel like the early-morning start was well worth it. Brockwell Lido is 50m long and wide enough to comfortably accommodate what feels like half of London in August. The water's unheated and there's no children's pool, but that doesn't stop kids wearing squeaky rubber armbands launching themselves into the water.

Wetsuited people can take up some of the pool doing triathlon training, but there's usually enough room for everybody. Thaw off at the brilliant Lido Café, set in a Grade II-listed art deco building; it does a mean latte and hearty breakfast. For members of Fusion (who operate the Lido), there's a spa complex attached to the pool with sauna, steam room and a hot jacuzzi to rest chilly bones after a dip.

—

Dulwich Rd, London SE24 0PA
Opening times: Weekends, 7:30am–9:30pm;
Monday to Friday, 6:30am–10pm; £3.20 adults
Getting there: ; ⊖ Brixton; ⇌ Herne Hill (train)
www.fusion-lifestyle.com/centres/brockwell-lido

🌸 FRENSHAM GREAT POND

On a hot day, tramping across the vast expanse of beautiful Frensham Common in Surrey, you'd be forgiven for thinking you were experiencing a mirage. The Great Pond is a dream come true for families, wild swimmers and sweaty hikers, especially those in the middle of the 13-mile Devil's Punchbowl route. Originally created to supply fish to the Bishop of Winchester's court, it's now popular with swimmers: part of the lake has been roped off to create a designated space for swimmers and the sandy shelf into the water is perfect for kids and families alike. The pond's water is fed by the River Wey and, although swimmers are advised not to swim further than the roped-off area (1.5m deep and 50m wide), it's too shallow for wild swimmers. On a quiet day, you may see people ducking out under the rope to thrash out some solid swims, although the council advises against this. There's a handy car park and small café on site to help you stay refreshed during a day at the beach. The area is a designated Site of Specific Scientific Interest, the Pond acting as a natural habitat for rare birds and to the silver-studded blue butterfly and a variety of dragonflies which dive in and out of the water and reed beds as you swim. Frensham Little Pond is run by the National Trust.

—

Situated between Farnham and Hindhead on the A287

Opening times: All day

Getting there: ⇌ Haslemere, then no. 19 Stagecoach stops opposite the ponds

✿ SERPENTINE LIDO

The Serpentine, a manmade pond in the middle of Hyde Park, feels like a far cry from the beach, but come summer, this is a pretty splendid place to cool off right in the centre of town. Famous for the Christmas Day dips when swimmers have to crack the ice with their fists to get into the water, the Serpentine only really opens its doors to members of the public from May onwards at weekends and then daily over the summer. The water fluctuates from a cool-to-properly cold spectrum, but it's such a brilliant location that plunging in after a day spent in a stuffy August office is magical. Open-water swimming is available in a 30 x 100m area and there's also a shallower pool for kids to splash around in. Wetsuits are permitted in the Serpentine, so you'll find your usual clutch of triathlon trainers smashing out the lengths, alongside more cautious swimmers relaxing with friends and family.

—

Opening times: May (weekends/Bank Holidays); 10am–6pm daily (June to August); £4.80 adults; £1.80 child; family ticket £12.00 (concessions apply)
Getting there: ⊖ Hyde Park Corner (Piccadilly), Queensway (Central)
www.royalparks.org.uk/parks/hyde-park/things-to-see-and-do/sports-and-leisure/serpentine-lido

Parks
Gardens
Secluded places
Wild London
Walks
Cycle routes
Water
Capital Ring
London Loop

A413

Chesham

A41

HATFIELD

A1(M)

M1

WATFORD

Borehamwood

HIGH WYCOMBE

120

A404

M40

MAIDENHEAD

M4

Windsor

M4

10

50

WEMBLEY

110

14

45

SEE PAGE 168

138

BRACKNELL

Egham

108

150

159

24

102

114

86

42

140

144

33

142

M3

A240

9

163   Frimley

161   Woking

135   Cobham

74

119

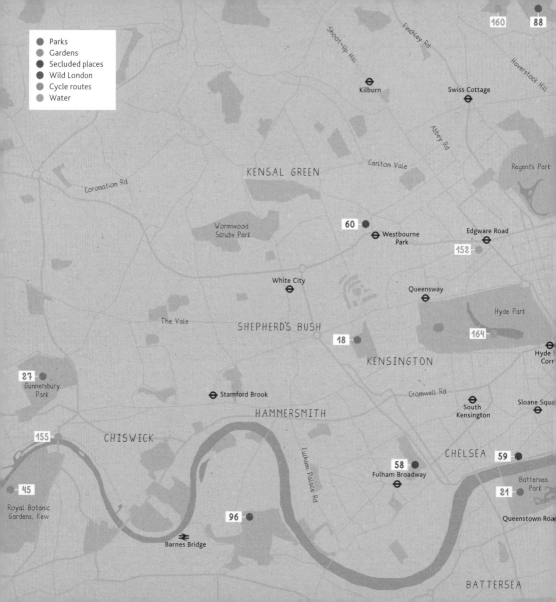

Legend

- Parks
- Gardens
- Secluded places
- Wild London
- Cycle routes
- Water

160

88

Shoot-Up Hill

Finchley Rd

Haverstock Hill

Kilburn

Swiss Cottage

Abbey Rd

Regent's Park

Carlton Vale

KENSAL GREEN

Coronation Rd

Wormwood
Scrubs Park

60

Westbourne
Park

Edgware Road

152

White City

Queensway

Hyde Park

The Vale

SHEPHERD'S BUSH

18

164

KENSINGTON

Hyde
Corr

27

Gunnersbury
Park

Stamford Brook

Cromwell Rd

HAMMERSMITH

South
Kensington

Sloane Squa

155

CHISWICK

CHELSEA

59

45

Fulham Palace Rd

58

Fulham Broadway

Battersea
Park

21

Royal Botanic
Gardens, Kew

96

Queenstown Roa

Barnes Bridge

BATTERSEA

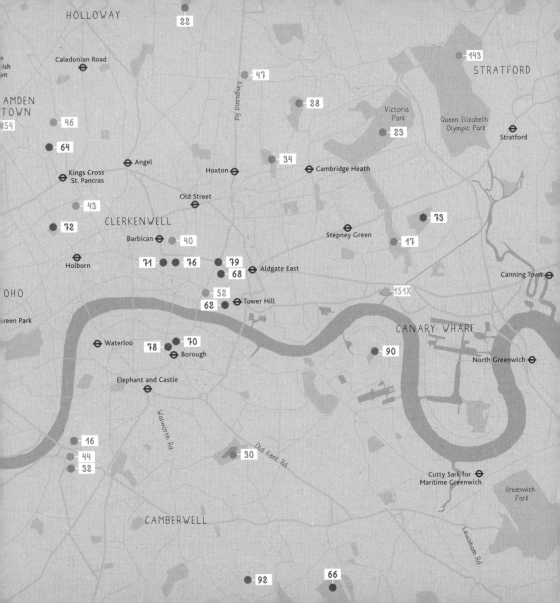

INDEX

First published in 2019 by White Lion Publishing,
an imprint of The Quarto Group.
The Old Brewery, 6 Blundell Street
London, N7 9BH,
United Kingdom
T (0)20 7700 6700 F (0)20 7700 8066
www.QuartoKnows.com

A catalogue record for this book is available from the British Library.

ISBN 978-0-7112-3997-5

Ebook ISBN 978-0-7112-4178-7

10 9 8 7 6 5 4 3 2 1

Design by Glenn Howard
Printed in China

Brimming with creative inspiration, how-to projects and useful
information to enrich your everyday life, Quarto Knows is a
favourite destination for those pursuing their interests and passions.
Visit our site and dig deeper with our books into your area of
interest: Quarto Creates, Quarto Cooks, Quarto Homes, Quarto
Lives, Quarto Drives, Quarto Explores, Quarto Gifts, or Quarto Kids.

MIX
Paper from
responsible sources
FSC® C104723